THE LONG WAY

HOME

An Autobiography

By Erni Burger

Copyright © 2002 by Erni Burger

ISBN 0-7414-1010-9

Published by:

PUBLISHING.COM

519 West Lancaster Avenue
Haverford, PA 19041-1413
Info@buybooksontheweb.com
www.buybooksontheweb.com
Toll-free (877) BUY BOOK
Local Phone (610) 520-2500
Fax (610) 519-0261

Printed in the United States of America

Printed on Recycled Paper

Published March, 2002

Dedication

Lovingly I dedicate "The Long Way Home" to my family and friends here in the USA and in Germany where I was born in 1926 and lived until 1948.

I'm sure there will be a smile or a few tears by some of us still around to remember. Thanks for being a part of my life.

TABLE OF CONTENTS

THE LONG WAY HOME

Selected from 75 years of my life

Part One: Germany 1926 – 1948
Part Two: USA   1948 – 2000

By Erni Burger

Acknowledgement

A warm thank you to "Spatz" which was the nickname for my husband Clarence who waited so patiently while I recalled my whole life story for three years. He and our son Mike lived just long enough to see my story completed. They both passed away shortly before this book was published.

Also to Teresa, the wife of our oldest grandson Benjie, for typing for me. To Kaylee, Teresa's sister, for helping with the editing. To Warren, a good friend, who recorded my story on tape. To Heinz, my brother-in-law from Germany for drawing the cover of my book. And to all the good people who encouraged me to write, "The Long Way Home."

I would also like to thank author David Irving for use of the pictures from his book *The Destruction of Dresden*.

Foreword

Marie Josephine Blei

"MAMA"

She was very important in my life. Maybe she was not as wise as she was pretty, or perhaps, she would have stayed in Luxembourg, where she was born in 1889. A nice little country where she fell in love with a German soldier named Otto Balling. Right after World War I they were married and started a new life in Baden-Baden, Germany, a well-known resort town on the edge of the Black Forest, where my life began.

Papa was a businessman, a happy and very likable man with big plans for the future. They had four children of which I was the youngest. There was Mimi the oldest, then Theo, Charlott and I.

Theo, Mimi, Charlott, and Mama

There were good times, I was told, but that would not last. Papa had joined a Glee Club. He had a very good tenor voice and was liked by many people.

Soon too busy for family life, our Papa started drinking too much. We were not told that he also cheated on Mama until much later. Mama closed the door on him forever. The papers show they divorced on the first of December 1927.

PART ONE

Germany
1926-1948

Chapter 1
My First Recollections

I was born the sixth of January 1926. A healthy baby with a name you would not believe. Erna Ida Gustava Balling. Somebody must have thought that I'd have gone far with names like that. Myself, I always hated them and later in life, dropped them all. Now, everybody calls me Erni.

I was a chubby little kid without a care in the world. Although, with leaner days ahead, I'm sure I lost weight. Anyway, Mama was in charge and she was dependable.

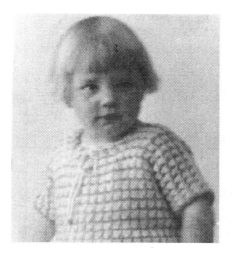

Mama had her problems all right. But she was a great pretender and never showed them. We were not to talk about our problems to anybody since it was nobody's business, so she always said.

I remember the white leather gloves she wore and the way she hand washed them in the evening, very gently. Every finger was stretched out with the handle of a wooden spoon and then laid on a folded bath towel to dry for the next day.

She always looked good when she went out and she was proud of us, since we were raised to behave. Mama often did not have a dime in her purse. Very few people

1

knew that we were poor and received help from the City of Baden-Baden for a long time.

We moved a lot and later I understood why. A respected place to live in was very important to her. Even though we lived in a rich city and were helped by it, the rent was sometimes too high. Mama had to look for something more reasonable to house her family.

I believe she enjoyed moving since she loved to decorate. Mama was talented in many ways. Anything that needed fixing, she could do herself. Watching her wallpapering was always fun. She could also repair plumbing and electrical things. One day she made us a new Fly-Cabinet for the pantry, in which we kept our food. She hated flies and not one of them was allowed to live with us for long. We did not have an icebox and a refrigerator was not yet heard of. Our Mama could do many things with very little money.

Papa lived with his new love. She was the daughter of a restaurant and dance hall owner. The Glee Club met there often. I saw her sometime later in life and could not understand how he would prefer her instead of Mama. She was vulgar and loud.

After he was married for a time, he tried to see Mama again, but she would not hear of it. He had two more children by then. She did not want him back. Occasionally he did come and ring the doorbell downstairs. We pretended not to be home. Sometimes Mama would put a dishtowel over the bell in the hall, so we could just hear a buzzing, dull sound. I thought that was funny at the time.

When I was five years old a little French boy downstairs invited all of us to his birthday party. All except Mimi, she was too old. We all went downtown in a motorcar to celebrate. I sat in the back by the window and hoped that everybody would see me. It was the first time I had ridden in a car.

I recall standing on a kitchen chair in a brand new dress that Mama had made. I was all set for elementary school, but not at all excited about it. Mama would walk me to kindergarten run by a Catholic sister named Alice, who I loved so very much. While I loved Sister Alice I wanted everything to remain just the way it was. We lived in a very nice house and I liked everybody in it – why'd I have to leave it for school?

Soon we were all in school and Mama was trying to find a job to make things better. She never found the kind of work she really wanted and ended up staying at home, making fancy lampshades for fine hotels and ladies that lived in villas. There were plenty of those in Baden-Baden. Making lampshades is not something just everybody could do. They were very time consuming, made with very small stitches by hand. They were made similar to the hats she used to create, when she was still in Luxembourg. To this day, I remember step by step how they were made with the frill they had in those days. When she was done it was a masterpiece to me. I must have been very interested in the things she'd done, since I remember them all so clearly. It was time again to move. I guess the city couldn't afford Mama's taste. Our new house was not far from where we'd lived. Way up under the roof, on the same street, only much smaller, and this time there was only one bedroom.

After Mama fixed it up, we all loved it there. We slept like the seven dwarfs from Snow White. Two beds together for Mimi, Charlott, Mama, and me. Theo slept in one smaller bed on the other wall. We had a living room with our nice furniture. We were not allowed in there, except on Christmas or other special days. There was a big bright kitchen toward the back. We lived there for a long time. It was also very close to school.

Front side of house
Living room and bedroom

We did have a few problems. Our lights would go out on occasion when we had no coin for the automat. It was located five flights down in the cellar. Then we had candles all over the kitchen. That was a fun time for me, but Mama could not work or sew. During those times we would listen to Mama read to us. When we ran out of books, she made up stories, which were even better. We also sang hundreds of songs, sad ones, funny ones, songs from our homeland and our God.

Backside of house

Our kitchen was quite large and very friendly. All the cupboards, table, chairs, and the big bench under the window, were painted with light green enamel paint. Each one of us girls had a private drawer in one of the cabinets for our personal treasures. Theo needed more room for his belongings. He had a stamp collection and was allowed to use the nice little cabinet with the shelf right under my drawer. It was not really private. Mama often snooped in everything and when she found it not in order, she would just turn the drawers upside down on the floor. When we came home we knew right away what that meant and straightened it up without comment. Mama was not mean exactly, but she had her little ways to tell us things without saying or getting mad at us.

I also remember her being a good cook. Even the simple meals were always tasty. In the summer she cooked on a portable two-burner gas stove. During the winter our wood stove was used for cooking and baking, mostly for Christmastime. Oh yes, it also had a water-tank built in for washing dishes. Mama kept that stove in very good shape. She sanded the top and kept the chrome polished. Yes, that stove was hard to move from house to house especially since it was very heavy and we always lived at the very top of the stairs. It was Mama's pride and joy, plus it kept our kitchen nice and cozy in the winter. Sometimes I long to see our old kitchen again. When we visited Germany, we drove to Baden-Baden and walked to the house we grew up in. Often, I feel like ringing the doorbell downstairs, the one that used to be ours. Now there are strange names on the nameplates, and I never had the nerve to push the button for the top floor on the right.

I did not like school very much. The teachers hardly ever smiled and they used different sticks to threaten us. They were not friendly at all and couldn't be pleased. Charlott was the smartest of us children. She did not like the teachers nor could she please them either, but she was the only one that was given a scholarship and that was hard to come by.

I remember wondering why my teachers always looked so angry. I wondered why they wore those long black skirts and black socks all the time, even in the summer. I also wondered if they were mothers. The thought gave me a chill. I was glad and thankful that I did not belong to one of them.

My teacher's name was Fraulein Stockel, which actually meant "little stick." That seemed so funny, since she always carried a long one. I decided I'd always give my Mama a big hug when I got home from school.

Chapter 2
Feeling the Change and Confusion

1933 was a very confusing time for me. Nothing made much sense. Mama did not care about political things so I could not understand why some people behaved as they did. But Mama didn't care, so I did not either. One day, somebody had given me an arm full of little paper flags. Some were all red with a hammer and a sickle on them. I also had little flags with swastikas. With no idea that I was doing something wrong, I started to decorate the fence by the house with one of these and one of those. It looked like a decoration for a parade, but a boy from the first floor came over and pushed me on the ground and then broke all my red flags. I was so hurt because I'd always liked that boy. Maybe it was mostly disappointment I felt. I remember running up four flights of stairs crying to tell Mama. She explained to me that it was voting time and that the two flags stood for two different beliefs. That is all she said except I should stay in the house for a few days. The next day all my little red flags where broken up and laying in the garbage can.

I liked the red flags because not long before all that happened, I went for a short time to a daycare center called, "The Red Falcons." I do not know where Mama had heard of it, but I liked it there. They had a big red flag. The people were nice and we always had a good lunch and learned new songs about the red falcons. Later I understood they were communists.

After the voting, Adolf Hitler was elected. He was our new Reichskonsoler. People said that from then on life would be better. Everybody would be able to find a job and Mama would be paid good money, since there was no father to take care of us.

We did live a lot better but we did have a lot more rules. Everybody talked about the good days ahead with our Fuhrer, Adolf Hitler. Most people liked him at that time.

7

My brother Theo was in the 8th grade. One day two
SS Olfiziers in uniform came to school and told them about
Hitler's top soldiers. They were looking for tall boys with
blonde hair and blue eyes. I do not know how tall they had
to be, but our Theo was not tall enough. He told us at home,
that one SS man said to the other, "This is what we want,
only a little taller." Theo was terribly disappointed. He was
hoping that he would have been one of the chosen. A few
years later though, we were all glad that he never was to be
one of those sharp looking SS men. They were trained to be
the most heartless and ruthless soldiers ever. Theo couldn't
hurt a fly.

Mimi, my oldest sister, had already finished three
years of training to become a beautician and was working on
her Master's degree. She was in charge of cutting our
fingernails, toenails, and our hair. She talked a lot about
what she would do with her first regular paycheck. First,
she bought herself a beautiful bicycle. That bicycle sparkled
in the sun with all the chrome and a light blue stripe. She
kept it clean and was so proud that she did not have to walk
that long way to work anymore.

After the bike, she did something crazy. She learned
the art of fencing. Oh, did she enjoy that, but not for long.
Even with Mama's help it couldn't be afforded very long. It
was a very expensive sport but still, she did it for a little
while and she had something to remember for the rest of her
life. Later, she gave me her white fencing dress. I wore it
for a very long time.

Our Theo had just graduated from school when he
did something for me that was so special. It happened in my
Home Economics Class in school when we were taught to
knit. Somebody made strange noises behind me with her
knitting needles. Everybody laughed, myself included. The
noise sounded very funny. Fraulein Blum, our teacher,
asked who had done it. However, nobody would tell. All
the girls on my side of the room, myself included, had to go
out front and open up our hands so she could hit them. She
hit them so very hard with her infamous bamboo stick, we all

cried out in pain. It was so unfair to all of us, except one, and she would not tell.

My hands felt like they were split in two. I came home and showed them to Mama and Theo. My hands had swollen to about twice their normal size. Mama and Theo looked very angry.

My hands were treated and I went to bed. The next morning in our classroom there was a knock on the door. I was called down to the principal's office. I did not know what it was all about. My regular teacher gave me that look like, "Now what have you done," and I was scared. When I got to the office, I saw my brother standing there, the principal, and Fraulein Blum. The principal asked me to open my hands. I had to tell him what had happened. My hands still had broken skin and were still swollen. My teacher was found guilty and was warned not to ever use that kind of stick again. She was to punish only the one proven guilty and that child was to stay after school. From that day on, my brother Theo was more than six feet tall to me.

Now that Theo was out of school, the rules had changed. All boys and girls had to do one year of special duty for twenty marks a month. Girls were placed in households to help mothers look after children, sick people, farms, actually wherever they were needed.

Theo was to go to a farm in Stuttgart. He replaced farmhands that had enlisted but he did not spend a whole year there, since it was more important for him to work in an airplane factory in Berlin. He was ready, even excited, to go to Berlin. It meant adventure and a big paycheck.

My friend Irmgart and I were always in trouble. It was not so terrible what we did, but hardly anything turned out just right for us. We stayed away from grownups as much as we could since they all had jobs for us to do. After school we went home first, changed our clothes, and found out if we could go and play for awhile and if so, for how long. We never had bad things in mind, but still ended up in trouble.

One day, we walked up a mountain road for no special reason and there, in the distance, we saw a little plum tree. It was so overloaded with plums that we just had to see it close up. The little tree stood about 50 feet or so from the road, in a meadow. We knew it belonged to someone close by. As we got closer, we noticed the ground all around the tree was covered with those little beauties. Since they were on the ground, we halfway hoped that it would be all right to take some. Both of us wore aprons, in which we gathered a few of them, when all of a sudden, there was the sound of a whistle, loud and strong. We knew then, such happiness was not to be. First, we walked slowly away, then by the count of three, we started running down the street to hide behind a garden gate. We stood still, breathing heavily from running. We didn't notice that the gate was up off the ground about a foot and a half and our shoes and legs were exposed. A man who'd followed us on a bike caught us. Not only did we give him back the plums, but we also told him our names, our teacher's name, and the name of our school.

Even though we decided to pray that night and did so, we were in trouble again the next morning in school. If only people would have talked to Mama instead, that would have been enough, but this way, the punishment would vary from the stick, to memorizing one of those long uninteresting poems that I just could not comprehend and that was so embarrassing.

We knew we were wrong and had talks about changing our ways. Were we different than the other kids or just unlucky?

Irmgart and I were both Catholic and good kids. At least we thought so. We went to the same church and never missed a Sunday Mass.

Then we thought we should do something special, to pay for our wrong doings. We gathered arms full of wild flowers in a meadow close by then went to church and started decorating.

I must say, we overdid it a bit. It was a beautiful church and very much cared for, but we were to do it even better. We had a good feeling while we worked all alone. It felt like being blessed already. Every statue was to have some of our beautiful flowers.

And then someone saw us. In no time at all there were many people there. Mostly women and of course our Chaplain was there. We had to clean up the "mess," as they called it. That must have been the biggest humiliation we ever had (from all our good deeds and there were many). That was the last straw. We knew what would happen the next day in school.

I remember we were sitting on an already cut woodpile, angry and disgusted, hopeless and ashamed. After awhile, we decided to just run away. Maybe we thought, even out of the country, maybe somewhere in Switzerland. Yes, we decided to go there no matter how far it was. It did not look so far on the map and they had the highest mountains there. We would be out of Germany, but still close enough to go home someday. Actually, we thought we could take one mountain at a time, as long as it was higher than the last, in time we would get there and that was the end of our conversation. We were both so angry and in a hurry to leave this place.

We both left a note. I wrote to Mama and told her what we had done and that we were going away. I grabbed a bottle of buttermilk from the Fly-Cabinet (Fliegenschrankchen) and a few other things. We never had anything very interesting in there.

I packed my knapsack and Irmgart came with a little squeaking suitcase with all kinds of good stuff like bread, cheese, and cookies. We left and walked up the same road where our plum tree story began and recalled all the misery. Oh yes, we were right. We had to go ahead with our plan. We walked a little faster until we came to the woods. There in a ditch along the street, we found little green frogs, hundreds of them. We played with them for a little while and then decided to have lunch (or was it supper?)

We did not know what time it was. We'd come a long way and were tired and hungry. The woods across the way didn't look too inviting. It must have been in the late afternoon and the woods were dark and damp. I think we were both changing our minds. I think I said something about a sweater. We didn't have a sweater or even a blanket. We agreed to go another time and we'd be more prepared. I think we ran all the way home. I don't know if Mama ever found out what we had set out to do.

From that day on I decided to spend more time at home. It was a lot safer there. I recall spending many hours looking out of the kitchen window. The large bench under it was just the right height for me to stand on. From there I had a good view no matter what time of year. There was always something going on down there for me to watch. During the winter snow, kids came with their sleds and rode down the little hill. Spring, Mama would plant beautiful geraniums and petunias in the window box, which was our garden there. Oh yes, the chestnut tree below the window was absolutely the largest and oldest one I'd ever seen. When it bloomed, it was the most beautiful chestnut tree ever.

One time, from the window I saw a gigantic airship, very slow and low flying. I called out so everybody could see it with me. Soon all the neighbors were watching this special event. I had the best view from way up there. "It is the Hindenburg," somebody said. We watched it until it was out of sight.

By this time, most young men were in the Army. We still thought we knew what Hitler was doing. He asked the people to trust him and we did.

Mama lived in her own world and did not get involved. We must have changed some and school was not the same any longer. I was the youngest in the family and still going. Now there was a lot of talk about our Fatherland and a lot of history and reasons why we all had duties to serve our country. Every subject had to do with our country's welfare.

One day our whole school had to go in groups to a farm close to the Rhine River to gather wheat that was left over, just lying around after the harvest. Our class alone gathered a few big sacks full of wheat so it would not be wasted.

Our arithmetic problems also had to do with our Fatherland. We had to figure out how many people lived in a square mile at that time. Since the population was increasing, how soon would we run out of room for our people? The answer was, that we just had to get back all the land, including the colonies that were lost in wars past, even if we had to fight for it.

There was a new rule now. It started in school. Instead of "Good Morning," we were told to raise our right arm and say, "Heil Hitler." Soon everybody did it everywhere except in church, I think. It was a strange thing to do. I wondered if the Fuhrer himself had ordered it. I felt it was something the Romans might say. Like "Hail Julius Caesar!" but we wouldn't say something like that out loud. It was hard to get used to at first. Later, you did not even know or care what you were saying, just so you did what was ordered. Mama just about got into trouble for mentioning that the milk was getting to be like white water.

Summertime arrived and it was a time we looked forward to. Six weeks of summer vacation from school. Ever since I was potty-trained, I had been going to camp, a place called the Sun Garden (Sonnen Garten). This camp was on top of a small mountain and built just for kids to have fun. It was run by two ladies who decided to do something special for children, and did they ever. I do not remember very much from my first visit, only a big sandbox and nice ladies. I was about 8 years old and I was the last sibling going there. I was happy to be there.

I was old enough to walk alone to the streetcar to meet my summer friends and the ladies in charge. When we arrived, we walked up the mountain like the many times before. It was a long way up but everyone was excited.

We started out with a nice breakfast and since it was the first day, we were all given a number to mark our blanket, pillow, playsuit, toothbrush, etc.

This year I hoped to get a full playsuit instead of just shorts. I was not developed like some of the other girls there, but I was afraid I would have to walk around without a top again.

When the garments came, and were passed out according to our age, I pretended I was busty enough by pushing out my rib cage. This time I made it. They gave me a big girls suit. I was okay. There were boys too, but in different buildings and we saw them only in the mess hall.

We got our bedding for nap time out of our own cubby for the summer (also numbered) and marched to a place under old trees to take a nap. Our cots were unfolded under the old fir and pine trees for a daily nap after dinner. We waited for the nice little man that brought us our food, promptly at noon. We always heard him coming up the hill with his horse and wagon, singing. I believe he was Italian. His eyes twinkled and he always had nice things to say when he saw us. His wagon was loaded with many shiny pots and cans and we all wondered, what was in them for us that day.

I often think of those two nice ladies that made all that possible. I dreamed that when I was old, and had a lot of money, that is what I'd do. We saw them both once a year. When the summer ended we always put on a show for them, right there outside where the cots were lined up. It was a most beautiful setting for an outdoor play. Afterwards, we had prize-winning games. They would say goodbye to every single one of us with a handshake. About 6 o'clock in the evening, we would walk down the mountain. I hated when summer was over.

Charlott had ended her schooling, plus one year of duty work, when she was looking for a nice paying job. She found one in Bruchsal, a nice little town about 35 or so miles away from Baden-Baden. She was hired right away to do office work in a large cigar factory. The owner and his wife liked her and since Charlott was still very young, they insisted on having her live with them, until she could make proper arrangements with Mama's consent.

Chapter 3
School Problems and my First Love

I was now 13 years old and had no more problems in school. Not that I loved it a whole lot, but I handled myself. Oh yes, I also had a boyfriend. No (in those days it was a nice name) a boy, that was also a friend. It was a nice friendship. We had so much to talk about. Things we were interested in and worried about. He was a good friend that cared and was fun to be with. I met him through a girlfriend about two years older than me.

We went to a very good ballet school together. It was a dream come true, just being accepted there. Elsa's friend Osi, a nice young man came with a friend named Biwi one afternoon to walk us home. Biwi was shy like me at first, but we became very good friends.

He must have told his mom and dad about me as I met them both. They were very nice. I liked them both very much and remember feeling very good about it, but I did not tell Mama just yet, since I was sure, that she would forbid my going to ballet class (which we could not afford anyway) plus the friendship with this boy.

But Theo found out about Biwi. He always spied on us girls. Maybe Mama asked him to? I'm not sure but I know she did not tell him to go and beat up my friend. Actually, neither of them were bullies, but in the progress of fighting they had hit each other bad enough. My friend ended up with a black eye and Theo had a swollen wrist. When I heard about it, I could have died. I was very embarrassed. I thought I could never forgive my brother for that.

The saddest thing about that incident was that they never got to see each other again. If Theo only had known how wrong he was, they could have been great friends.

Mama couldn't afford ballet class anymore, but I was grateful, while it lasted and just like Mimi, when she had her chance to go to fencing school, I have those memories too for the rest of my life. Now, that I think of it, Mama wanted it that way and even though she couldn't let us continue, she tried. That's the way she was.

Christmas was near. Mimi was married now and had a baby, a beautiful little girl. Her name was Lotti. Theo and Charlott came home and we all knew in our hearts, that this Christmas would most likely be our last one together. Mama was always known by us to be the best in creating the true Christmas spirit to celebrate our Christmas Eve. Like I said before, we were seldom allowed in the living room, and from October on, that room was locked. She used the living room for her workshop since she made most of the gifts. Mama was busy, making things for Christmas. She made cookies, candies, and whatever was stored there for Christmas Eve.

All of our toys were stored in the attic during the year. People Mama worked for gave us beautiful things. There was no room for clutter during the year since we had only a kitchen and that had to be picked up at all times.

But when Christmas was near, we could depend on seeing all our things. She brought it all down and got busy. My dolls were newly dressed and cleaned up so they looked brand new again. My dollhouse was put up. This was no ordinary house like we know here. There were two rooms side

16

by side with a swinging door in the middle. It also had a window in each room with curtains. There was miniature furniture and the floor and table lamps were battery operated. The kitchen had a little stove that could be used to cook on and a sink with a faucet that actually worked and was supplied with water from a container outside the house wall. Everything was very well made. There were also miniature dishes, pots and pans, and silverware and whatever else was needed in the kitchen.

My brother had a toy store with his name on it, in big letters. It had a roof on it just like the little shops at the Christmas market by the old church in town. It had a little side door for the storekeeper and a little seat. The front was half open, with a counter built in. It looked like a firecracker stand but nicer and much smaller and was filled with all kinds of goodies. One year his store even had real mini sausages on a long string that were attached across the front.

We all had play money and could buy there. Theo was always munching while he sold us things. When Mama was at work in the living room, she was full of ideas. I remember one Christmas Eve when we waited in the kitchen on the other side of the door on a blanket. Mama rang the silver bell (which I still have) and then we were to come in. This was the year we celebrated our last Christmas together.

No toys, no frills, just a few things we needed, like my brown rubber boots I'd finally got after hoping for a number of years. They were simple but nice. They looked like riding boots. There was only one problem. During the winter when I needed them most, my feet got ice cold just like Mama had told me. This year I got them anyway. "Just because."

This year Christmas was different. Theo had to build a manger for Mama's Christmas project. It was made for our new Christmas baby Lotti. The manger was regular height and was placed under the Christmas tree. It had straw inside and a soft piece of cloth, on which little Lotti was laid. When the little silver bell rang and we all entered the room, we saw her first. It was so simple and beautiful that we all had tears in our eyes. Lotti had big brown eyes and while we all looked at her, we saw a tiny reflection of a burning candle in them from the tree branch above.

That Christmas was completely different. But I am sure, that none of us in the family has ever forgotten. Mama had done it again.

Right after Christmas everybody was packing up their things to leave. Theo back to Berlin; Charlott to Bruchsal where she now worked; Mimi, Heinz, and little Lotti to Uckermunde in Pommem, as far east as you can go in Germany.

Now there was just Mama and I at home. Charlott had mentioned she'd found a nice apartment in Bruchsal and asked if we would like to come live there. We talked about it and decided to go see it.

The house in Bruchsal was grand. It was right next to the Castle Garden on a quiet and respected street. It was built in the same style as the castle. It must have been built about the same time with the same pink sandstone and old paintings on the front wall.

It was very exciting for me to think we might get to live there. Of course, upstairs under the roof again, as always. It was once used for servant quarters but could be fixed up very nice with a little imagination, and the price was right. We decided to rent it right then and there. We could never afford what we had in mind to do with it, but just living there was great.

Just coming up that beautiful stairway, made you feel special. At the time there was a big chandelier way up on the ceiling for light, to the three apartments. I remember how quiet I used to pass the two apartments below us. It was not a place to take two steps at one time when you were in a hurry.

Charlott was in love with the boy next door. After we lived there for a short time I saw him often going out of his gate on his bike. He was a nice young man and very good looking. I decided he was good enough for my sister. He was tall, handsome, dressed well, and played tennis. But he also played the violin, constantly, and sometimes got on my nerves when he practiced.

Later, I found out that he was very good. In fact, he was the first violinist to play in the castle orchestra. I saw him once in royal blue velvet and white powdered wig when he played right there under the balcony on the back entrance (see picture). There were lanterns everywhere and ladies and gentlemen in costumes walking in the park. Bruchsal is small but it has lots of charm.

Chapter 4
So Many Orders

My friend Biwi from Baden-Baden had decided to come to Bruchsal to see me. He told me so on a postcard. He knew where I lived and would arrive about 5 p.m. and wait for me on a bench in the park, that I could see from the back window. But Mama found the card and I had to confess.

I was very worried about what I should do. I was given a theatre ticket for the same time and Mama insisted that I go since it was a gift for me from the mother of Charlott's boyfriend next door. Mama said that she would check on my young man waiting at the bench and tell him the time of my return. It was such a surprise to hear her say that. She talked more like a friend then my Mama. I thought it was so nice of her, I felt she actually cared about my problems.

The play was so long and I could not concentrate on it. It had started to rain real hard. In my mind, I saw my friend waiting for me on the bench, getting drenched. I was sure that Mama had forgotten all about it. Before I went into the house I checked the bench, but he was not there. When I came home, Mama opened the door and pretended that she had forgotten all about my friend in the park.

I was so upset and disappointed that Mama acted so cruel. I felt so bad. I never forgot the day she opened the living room door. My boyfriend was right there all along. I must have looked bad. I was so very upset, disappointed in Mama, and angry and now, ashamed too. It was terrible. I did not think it was a funny trick. Mama explained that it was supposed to be a surprise, but it was hard to be happy right away.

They were both drinking coffee and there was a cake that was not in the house when I left. How it got there, I don't know. I meant to ask but never got around to it. Everything turned out okay. Later, Mama made a real good meal and for once, Mama was sorry. I could tell she'd had a powerful talk with my friend while I was gone and found out that I was right about my suspicions.

The future did not look very good. Everybody knew it, but was afraid to talk about it out loud. It seemed all young men were either in the Army or working for the coming war. Theo was still in Berlin building airplanes but did not know for how much longer.

Mimi was homesick and wanted me to come and live with her for a while. I packed my suitcase, my friend Biwi came to say goodbye. We spent a nice day together but we had mixed feelings about my going away. I wonder if we all had the same thing in mind. Biwi carried my suitcase and hardly talked. We said goodbye again, while I was already on the train. I started to feel real sad leaving them all behind but we all promised to write to each other.

After they were out of sight, I started thinking about my long trip all by myself and soon I was not sad anymore. It was going to be my first big adventure. I was excited again and soon I would see Mimi, Heinz, and Lotti and the new baby boy also called Theo. It was a long trip. I never imagined I was going so far away from home.

When I arrived and stepped from the train looking for Mimi, I noticed about eight young people about my age and a small group of ladies. Mimi was among them. They all welcomed me. That was a nice surprise. We walked to a small village. It seemed everybody knew I was coming.

The town was very small like I said. Some people, actually most of them, still had outdoor toilets and pumps for their water. That was hard to get used to. No wonder Mimi was homesick.

Mimi and Heinz had a nice beauty shop. I believe it was the only one in the village at the time. They lived in a small but pleasant apartment.

Mama had sent us presents for Christmas, which was great. I got a real nice record player and a few of my favorite records. It was a little portable one that wound up. It came in a small black suitcase, and was very modern for that time.

When I first saw it, I could not believe that it was to be mine. I don't know how Mama did it and it had to cost her. I was stunned. The only thing was, I couldn't find the needle for it and I was frantic. I laid it aside and was so disappointed that I couldn't play my record. Then an idea hit me. I found a sewing needle, cut the point, and used it.

I knew it was not good for my records but I could hear it very scratchy and faint, that's when I found the needles. They were located in a chrome corner of the case that had to be pushed out. It was great. I didn't know what all was in the box for everybody else. I was too excited to care at the time. After the holiday, I finished my schooling there and stayed until the following Christmas.

I loved my new schoolteacher. She was so interesting to listen to and so understandable that it was great fun to learn.

It was time to go back home. I felt sorry for Mimi. She was so homesick and could not go home with me. All my new friends walked me back to the train. I felt so good and I had a lot of stories to tell at home. Plus, I finished school with good grades.

It was good to be back home again. War had started and ration cards were given to everyone. My boyfriend Biwi had to go to war and ended up in Africa. We wrote to each other for a long time. Including the time he became a prisoner of war and was shipped to Ottowa, Canada. I knew he would be safe until the war ended.

Theo was living in Berlin and had found a place for me to do my year of duty (pflicht jahr). It was close to where he

23

lived and Mama approved. I packed again to go to a little town close to Berlin to work in a bakery where help was needed since husband and son had gone to war.

There was a lot of work for me and I liked it. The only problem was there was nobody to talk to and I was so far from home. The owner was a nice lady but for some reason I had to sleep on the living room couch. Why, I don't know, because it was a big house.

The work I had to do was not hard. I was lonesome after work and sometimes on Sunday when Theo did not come. I remember one of those Sundays I was waiting for Theo and wondering if he had forgotten me. I was standing by the window waiting, when I saw him coming. I flew out of the house to greet him. He could see how I felt and asked all kinds of questions. How much I had to do did not bother him, but when he asked me to show him my room and I told him about the couch in the living room, he asked me where my suitcase was and I packed again. I was not to stay there. It was after I told him I had to wait until everybody was out of the living room before I could go to sleep, Theo said I had a very good reason to leave under those circumstances. Then he found the lady. She looked surprised and said she had no idea that I was not happy there. We said goodbye and left.

Theo had a little room close by with a nice landlady. He told her what had happened. She fed us both and showed me a room where I could sleep until I found another place to work.

Not long after that, Theo came home from work, got on his bike to take me to another place. Oh boy, what a trip that was. I had to sit on the bar in front, sideways, and my suitcase tied to the back. How we ever made it all the way there I don't know, but it was worth it. I was closer to Berlin in Blankenfelde. My job was now at a big nursery with many greenhouses, flowers, and vegetables everywhere.

They already had a girl like me from Berlin. We had a nice big room together and we got along real well. We learned a lot there, which was of much use for us later in life.

It was a very interesting job. Even in the winter when bulbs and seeds were planted and repotted some two and three times until they were ready for market. We turned the soil with spades, pulled weeds, sprayed and watered everything daily.

More and more our lives were in danger. Many nights were spent sitting in the cellar listening to bombs exploding over Berlin. At first, we all huddled together, we were terribly afraid. After a while, we just prayed quietly.

Many nights we listened to the falling bombs and we prayed for all of the people there. We also heard our glass panels in the greenhouse being broken by shrapnel. We knew we would have to repair them the next morning.

Two prisoners of war came to help us. Their names were Etienne and George. They were two young family men that longed to go home. They came from Lion and Bordo, France. It was really not too bad for them. We had a good life compared to many. They were treated just like family and had good food. Trucks would bring them each morning and picked them up each night.

We were allowed to talk to them but had to be careful of what we said. George, the younger one was very homesick, and we could tell when he was really homesick because he would sing sad songs while he worked.

One day while working side by side at the potting table, George asked me if I would help him to go home to

France. All I had to do was bring him a roadmap and traveling clothes. It really was hard turning him down. I knew he could never escape. We both could have lost our lives for something like that. Still, I hope and pray they both made it back home safely.

Other than working, eating, and going out with my brother once in awhile, there was not much to do on Sundays.

A new girl was hired. I didn't like her. However, it so happened that my brother did. I am not sure, but I think he had met her long before and helped her to get the job.

One day, she had my record player. She insisted that Theo had given it to her as a present. He'd borrowed it from me sometime before and always forgot to bring it back. First I was hurt and then I got mad. Very mad! Especially when she played my records.

I asked for permission to go to Theo's place right after we were paid our monthly twenty marks. Theo was not at home yet, but his landlady gave me permission to wait in his room. I waited a long time. It was getting late and I had to leave soon. I decided to write him a note and tell him what I thought of him. Oh boy, did I tell him. There was a little stove in his room already lit and stoked. When I saw him come in smiling, I lost my nerve and very quickly crumbled up the note and tossed it in the fire along with my twenty marks. I'd had it in my hand, I don't know why it was out of my purse or what I had in mind for it, but I confessed quickly. Theo tried to retrieve it fast, but it was too late. The note and my hard earned money went up in flames. His hand and arm were burned badly. I still hated him but he'd been punished enough. We bandaged his hand and arm. He felt a little better and was sorry for what he had done. He promised to buy me another record player even better in red leather, one he had seen somewhere. I know he meant it, but it never happened.

Right after the year was over and I was free to go home, we all said our goodbyes and wished each other good luck.

I was again on my brother's bike and soon on the train home. Mama decided to stay with my oldest sister Mimi.

Theo stayed in Berlin. Now I could plan my own life. I'd waited for that day long enough.

What would I do first? For a while, I lived with Charlott, which was nice. However, I also knew I could be a burden to them, which I did not want. I decided to go to Business College for a short time and then find myself a job. All the way home I planned my life.

Charlott and Heinz were at the train to meet me. They now had a little girl named Christa and they really wanted me to stay with them and agreed with my plans. I learned to type, shorthand, filing, etc. and after I knew how to do that, I found myself a job. It was a job Mama would not have approved of, but it paid good and sounded like a lot of fun.

Chapter 5
My First Job (Lonely Hearts)

I decided to find out about a job in the "lonely hearts business." I'd help find a partner for everyone that was lonely. First, I went to find out what it was like. I decided to take the job, since all I had to do was type and file.

At 6 a.m., I had to take the train to Karlsruhe first. Then a long streetcar ride plus a few minutes walk. I was used to getting up early in Berlin and what I had to do, was simple enough to start.

There were light blue and pink files for male and female. I had to put an ad in the weekly paper and then people would come to see us to sign up. We introduced them according to their choices, until they met the right partner.

Anybody could start a business like that. There were many lonely and shy people in the world. It was simple and it paid well plus, we made a lot of people happy (I hope). I loved my job and was good at it, if I say so myself. Even the long daily trips didn't bother me, especially since I traveled first class.

It was a little strange for me to be deciding for myself. However, Mama was not there and Theo was not to check on me anymore. I don't want to sound ungrateful, but I was ready to be on my own.

There was Charlott if I needed advice but she trusted me. She made me welcome in her home and we never had any problems. There were rules and I kept them. Many times I asked her if she preferred I left, to live somewhere else. Whenever I talked about it, she would say, "Why? You like it here don't you?"

Once, my boss left for a few days and I found myself alone in the office. There was nothing special planned for me to do. I answered the telephone and typed letters from the basket. When the doorbell rang, a nice and proper gentleman told me he was there to meet a young lady. I asked him into the parlor to wait until I found out whom he was to meet and when. Well, it happened there was no other explanation, except that my boss had told this gentleman, now sitting in the other room, to be there but not the lady in question.

I called her right away and she was surprised since nobody had informed her of this meeting. She was not prepared and could not come right away. She also mentioned the beauty shop and the long trip to our office.

I was frantic as to what I should do. This was something I never had done before. After I found his blue file and read it, I grabbed a pink file at random of another lady that lived in town. I remembered her age was right. I called her; she was ready to come right away. Now all that took a little time. I checked on the gentleman in the next room and I saw that he was a little annoyed since he had waited so long. I explained what had happened and what I had done. He seemed amused. He was game and waited a bit more. By the time she had arrived at our office, I was a nervous wreck. I introduced them to each other and I left the room, leaving them to themselves. I hoped for the best. I had things to do, but I couldn't concentrate on anything. I paced the office floor wondering what would happen next. I also worried about what I had done and whether I would get away with it.

After what seemed a long time, there was a knock on my office door. I opened it and all I could see were two heads, sort of on top of each other. They were smiling and thanked me and left. I watched them from my window, walking away arm in arm and I felt pretty good.

After my boss came back from wherever he was (a wedding most likely), I told him my story. He just laughed and could not understand why this lady had considered meeting that man since he was not what she was looking for, according to her file.

A few months later, the same couple was married. I hoped they lived happily ever after. I was always interested in meeting new people and enjoyed my work there. However, about a year later I decided to quit. Bombs were falling everywhere and trains were often attacked as well. I felt like going home and finding a new job. Bruchsal was still much safer. It was a much smaller town and other than a large railroad station there was nothing interesting that somebody might do away with.

Chapter 6
Trained for Hospital Work with the Airforce

I applied for a new job in Bruchsal. I was told I had only two choices, hospital or clerical work in the Armed forces. I decided to work in a hospital filling out the papers. I was in the Airforce now and ordered to go to Starmberg for training. Starmberg was a beautiful town right by a lake. When we arrived, I saw a little old castle near the water. That was where the boys were to be trained as medics. The girls lived up on the hill in barracks. There we were assigned to one room with five bunk beds for ten girls. From this time on we were soldiers and treated as such. We learned to march and obey all the rules. Each morning we would fall in and march down past the castle to an area by the water. We sat in a half circle, and waited for our teacher. He was a young doctor dressed smartly in an Airforce uniform.

We had a lot to learn in a short time. The sound of a whistle was what we lived by from then on. We were absolutely not allowed to speak to any boys from the castle. But in the evening, when we were all in our bunks after bed check, we talked about them.

There was one fellow everybody noticed and wanted to meet outside the gate on a Sunday. I listened, but since I had a boyfriend in Africa, I really was not interested. We all had passes on Sunday. We could go wherever we wanted, just so we were back through the gate by 10 p.m.

Starmberg was serene and beautiful. Most of us would go there on our day off. There were many nice souvenir shops and small cafes and if you had your ration card, you could enjoy a nice piece of cake.

Hildegart, a nice roomy from Karlsruhe, and I were good friends right away and always returned together.

One Sunday we were tired of walking. I sat by the edge of the lake and took off my shoes to cool my feet. Suddenly, the neat looking fellow everybody talked about was behind me asking if I was all right. I really don't believe he thought I had a foot problem, but he sat down with us. We talked and spent the rest of the day together. He was a nice fellow. His name was Gunther Wild from Dresden. He had just started medical school when he was called into the Army to become a medic.

We liked each other's company and decided to write to each other. There was a mailbox right by the castle. We didn't need a stamp to mail our letters. We just went there at a certain time and exchanged our letters.

This went on for some time. We saw each other on Sundays in Starmberg and we would walk or rent a rowboat. Sometimes we rowed across the lake to investigate whatever there was to see. We just had to be sure that we were back by 10 p.m.

One time we decided to see Munchen (Munich) close by and for some reason missed our train on the way back by just a few minutes. We went to see the city and had gotten lost for a while. We got back 35 minutes late. That was a big deal. For our punishment, we both had KP the next two Sundays. My roommates found out and started pulling all kinds of tricks to get me in more trouble. I figured they were jealous. After awhile, we were all friends again.

When our schooling came to an end, we were all assigned to different countries, mostly Greece. I was one of the younger girls and needed permission from my parents to leave the country. Mama would not sign, as I was just about to leave for Athens, Greece.

After talking to Gunther, who was also going to Athens, Greece, he said, "Why not try to go to Dresden. Working in a hospital is a lot better and safer for a girl." He wanted me to meet his mom and see the beautiful city, Dresden.

Hildegart wanted to go wherever I went. That was not easy but our Doctor (Oberarzt) made it possible for us. There was one problem. Dresden was not in our jurisdiction and Baden-Baden by Wien was. So we both had to relocate to Berlin first to have our assignment approved.

34

I never liked big cities and Berlin was very confusing for us. We did find the place and were assigned to Dresden Nickern, a small hospital right next to a big Luftwaffen Technical School, on top of a hill, outside of the city.

With orders in our packet, and too much luggage, we were traveling again. We were tired after all the excitement. I couldn't sleep, however Hildegart had no problem. I started to think about all kinds of things. It was a long trip to Dresden. Our Theo was now a soldier in Russia somewhere. Would he be coming back home to us when all this was over? Where was everybody from my family and how were they?

Bombs were falling here and there. If only I could put it all out of my mind like Mama was able to do. Why do we have gas masks? They were given to us in Starmberg. We were to keep them but hadn't gotten our uniforms yet. Somebody would do something about that. After all, we were not meant to be in Dresden. Hopefully, nobody knew about us.

It was a little funny to think how we got to be there at all. My mind just wandered while Hildegart slept so soundly beside me. I remembered our last get-together when Theo had come home for a short time just before he'd gotten orders to join the army.

It was nice for a little while and then Theo had to leave. It had been quite a long time and I had not heard of him since. Mama was upset, but Theo talked her out of it by changing the conversation. I thought about my brother in Russia somewhere. Oh my God, what is going to happen to us all?

As we got close to Dresden, somebody called for us to get ready. I woke up Hildegart and we took our suitcases down and waited. When we came out of the train station, we saw Dresden, what a beautiful city. The city had not been bombed. There was no sign of war here and best of all we'd be able to sleep at night without interruption.

People told us there was no industry or anything warlike there to bomb. Many went there because they had lost their homes in other cities. They believed they would be absolutely safe there. There was no military except the Luftwaffen Technical School way outside of Dresden and we were going there. First, we took a streetcar. We then transferred to a bus that wound through the country. The last part of the journey, we walked up a hill carrying our luggage. I remember losing my hat when a rainstorm came. We had to run after it through the fields. We laughed many times about chasing my hat.

Upon arriving, to the left we saw large buildings, which had to be the school. On the right was a gate where we had to show our papers to get in. Then we saw our new home, a little hospital. Further up the hill stood rows and rows of barracks, which looked empty.

We must have looked terrible when we arrived and walked into the waiting room. We were carrying our suitcases and were wet and exhausted. There were many patients waiting for their turn. Oberarzt Dr. Sauer, our new boss came out and looked surprised to see us. We introduced ourselves and showed him our orders. He realized that we'd walked all the way up the hill in the rain and assured us that no one had told him about us and therefore, hadn't sent anybody to pick us up. Then he called a medic to carry our belongings up to the first barrack where we picked a room, cleaned up, and got ready to report for duty.

We did not have a uniform yet, since we did not go through the proper channels, but he was very easy to talk to. Dr. Sauer smiled and gave us two of his white gowns to wear. He was a big man and his gowns were large but we did what he said looking very ridiculous for a while. We never did receive proper uniforms since we'd been displaced but we received smaller gowns instead. Dr. Sauer told us to look around until he was through with his patients. We found five bedrooms with six beds each, a little lab, tea kitchen, a little office, bathroom with showers, and one empty room that was to be for physical therapy. We talked to the few patients there. Nobody at that time was very sick, just minor injuries, rashes, or ingrown toenails, etc. I could handle that; it just so happened that we both had never yet seen a real sick person or someone seriously hurt or dead.

Our doctor came and we talked about duties. He was not hard to please. He just wanted what we did, done right. He told us that we'd have a lab technician soon. He had just started there and wanted all of us to make it a little hospital we could be proud of.

The next morning we knew exactly what to do. By the time the doctor came to make his rounds, we had the patients washed; beds made; temp, pulse, and blood pressure taken; and whatever else he had ordered. He'd said he was very satisfied with us and that was good to hear. The waiting room was always filled with patients. He was a very good doctor and worked hard to build up this little hospital. Soon he was transferred and replaced by Stabsarzt Dr. Muller whom I considered the best doctor. He was a little older and was like a father to us, as long as we did everything right. He also had a way of letting us know when we did not meet his expectations. His wife and two little boys lived just down the hill and I babysat the boys once in awhile. We all felt as if we were part of his family.

I had received training to give massages and therapy. Dr. Muller appointed me in charge of the physical therapy room. There were a few prisoners of war soldiers working in the kitchen next door. Whenever one of them came for treatment, Dr. Muller would tell me, "Let them sleep for an hour or so under the heat lamps then turn it off and let them rest." He did not like Hitler.

We all knew that even though, he didn't come right out and say so. Some mornings when he felt really good he would make jokes about the man that was running our country. He would get off his noisy motorcycle, come in real peppy and say something like, "So, we lost the last war, you wait and see, we are going to win this one too. Now lets get started."

A few times our sirens were used to alert us that enemy airplanes were overhead. We could actually see them but they kept on going and Dresden slept on. We started digging single manholes in the fields close by just in case. I dug my whole much bigger since I babysat Dr. Muller's little boys now and then.

Heavy bombers flew over us more and more and we kept wondering which city would be wiped out next.

It seemed like the whole world went raving mad around us. After they flew by we would go back to work.

Chapter 7
Total Confusion

Theo wrote me a letter from Russia about this time with photos of him somewhere on the way to Moscow. They were stuck and out of gas. It was so sad to see all those pictures in the bitter cold. I couldn't help worrying about him. What in the world did those boys have to do in a big country like Russia? I know I am not very smart, but to think that little Germany tried to fight every country around us was idiotic.

Theo did not say more about his situation. He was writing because of a letter he received from Mama. She was thinking of getting married again. She wanted to know what he thought about it first. Theo asked me to write to her right away and tell her that we are all happy for her. Mama needed somebody to be with and take care of her. It was all he said except that he was praying more lately and that I should wish him good luck.

I did write her and in her next letter she asked me to get permission from Dr. Muller to let me come home for awhile. I was so surprised that he could arrange a pass for a whole week.

When I arrived home, Charlott was there with little Christa. She had arrived from Bruchsal to meet Mama's new husband. Charlott's husband was also somewhere in Russia and Mimi could not come. Travel was too risky at that time.

After we met our new stepfather, I was not sure if I liked him. Mama assured me he was a good man. We were told that Mr. S was in the wine business and was active in the black market since he had the wine to trade.

That did not bother me. I never thought that it was so terrible to trade something I had for food when I was hungry. More and more, marks were worthless.

Mr. S., now my stepfather, offered me money for each good painting I could find. He kept telling me that Dresden was full of collectibles.

I tried, but that was something to worry about and to spend time on, which I didn't have enough of. Also, anyone could tell that I didn't know prices. I would send them home never to know if they would get lost or damaged on the way there. I had better things to do with my spare time.

One day, probably a Saturday, I was walking through town and noticed a sign that said "Heimbau Niedersaxen." It was a bank where you could save for a down payment on a new little house. I went in, there were many plans, each different. I looked at them many times and wondered if anything like that would be possible for me.

There was a nice older man. He explained how it could be done. He said if I was interested in saving for one of those little houses and were willing and able to pay a certain amount every payday he could guarantee that I was on the way to owning one someday. He also made it clear that there was a guarantee that I could never lose my money. Later though I lost it anyway – all of it.

By now everything was routine. I was surprised one day when I looked at my ration card, that I was to get a pack of cigarettes. That was strange. I did not have anybody to trade them for something else, so I smoked them. Someone had told me it would keep me from being hungry all the time but that is not so.

Then we were asked to give blood for a small piece of salami. Like I said, small but delicious. I gave too much blood and fell out of my shoes one day and was not allowed to give anymore.

One day word got out that close to us was a farm with potatoes still in the ground. One night with a flashlight I went to dig some. They were still very small. I also found some nettles, which was supposed to be full of iron and taste like spinach.

I had night duty and went to the kitchen and started to peel my potatoes. The doctor came in and saw what I was doing. I told him how I got them. He looked at me like he did not approve of that at all. But, he must have changed his mind because he came back with a handful of cocoa butter suppositories.

He fried the potatoes while I made my nettles spinach. The potatoes were very good but the spinach we just could not eat. That was the last time I gathered nettles. They were murder on your hand and tasted very bad. I had to promise never to repeat that again and did not, but wanted to many times.

I got sick one day and the doctor told me there was no mistake, I had diphtheria. This sickness was not heard of for a long time. I had it, and so did many other people. I believe it came from war circumstances like unsanitary conditions after bombings. I could be wrong, but it seems to me that typhoid, tuberculoses, diphtheria, even the black plague broke out after many people were killed and not buried right away.

I ended up in a large hospital in Dresden and was there for a long time and nearly died. When I started to get better, they put me in quarantine. We were bedded down in a large room with iron bars on the windows until all three tests showed negative.

I had a letter from Mama. She found out about me. She said that there was a large basket with food on the way for me. That was wonderful news. We were starving here. My friend Hildegart never did come to see me while I was in the hospital and I could understand why. Diphtheria is a very contagious illness. However, I felt she could have called me to see if I was still alive.

Dorle, a very special and nice girl was laying in the bed next to me. Many times she shared fruit, bread, whatever she had. Her mom came each day to see her through the glass. I had told her about my big basket from home and that we both would have a big feast. My basket never came and Dorle went home, since all three of her tests were negative. I felt so bad before she left, but we promised each other to stay in contact.

And then one day it was my turn to leave that terrible place. First I went home to our room where Hildegart and I lived in private quarters. It was close to work and much nicer then the barracks which soldiers occupied at that time. I found my big basket with Mama's handwritten labels on the jars. They were not cleaned yet, so I could still smell them even though they were totally empty.

Mama had outdone herself. She cooked and canned a whole rabbit. It was gone as well as the jelly. A coffee cake that Mama baked – gone, everything gone. I could smell the paper to know that there was also salami. I could not believe what she went through to get all that together. It was just incredible. How could I thank her for it and not tell her?

Angry and hurt, I ran up the hill to the little hospital and told on Hildegart. Dr. Muller was just like a father to us. It came very natural to me to do that.

He listened and then told me to forgive her and to try to forget it and best not to talk about it anymore. He also said we were soldiers now and if the story got out, Hildegart could be in trouble. After all, he said that food was there whenever she came home. It must have been a big temptation for her.

I could understand what he was saying, but all of it? From that day on I only talked to her when I had to. Hildegart never apologized, ever. Dorle was my best friend now and I moved all the way to Dresden.

It took a long time to totally forgive Hildegart, but more and more I could see that Stabsarzt Dr. Muller was right.

I found a room in a very fine neighborhood in Dresden. It was a long way to work for me every morning but I liked my new home a lot. I lived with two very old respected people in a small villa, a judge and his sister. My room was on the second floor and had a balcony toward the back. From there I had the prettiest view of the garden. We lived not far from the train station in the Radezki Strasse, which I passed every morning on the way to work. I had to walk about a fifteen minutes to catch the streetcar.

The house itself seemed very dark inside. There were a lot of dark old paintings everywhere, especially on the long staircase wall. It was so quiet all the time. I was not allowed any visitors, which was sad. I would like to have shown it to my friend Dorle.

I was invited to Dorle's house many times though. It was a happy house. We all had good voices and sang a lot. Dorle (Dorothy) had a sister. She sang in the opera house. She taught us numerous songs (whenever I hear them now on my favorite classical radio station, it reminds me of those days).

The food situation was about as bad as is could get but Dorle's mom always set the table with flowers. You felt as if you were going to a special formal party. Sometimes, we ate (on beautiful Dresden china), a slice of bread with margarine and red and white radishes all cut into little roses. It was just incredible with fancy napkins and lively conversation. They were the most beautiful family I had ever met.

Mama came to visit unexpected. She was on her way home to stay there for a while. It was such a happy surprise, but she was only allowed to spend one night with me. From then on I did not think so highly of my landlady anymore. I am sure that she would never have rented a room if she did not have to.

There were many people in Dresden now. More and more arrived every day to find a home. Anybody with more room than what they needed was asked to share.

Dresden was known by now to be a promised land for the homeless. Nobody knew why, but it was never bombed. One day, I heard somebody say, "Maybe the enemy keeps it safe for themselves once the war is over." You could say those things but never very loud. I always liked to think because it was so beautiful.

I had a lot to do on my days off. Dresden had to be seen. Everywhere you went you discovered new wonders. There was so much to be seen and free of charge.

Once a week I went to school, evening classes. I do not exactly know why, but I ended up in Berliz School. You can find them everywhere in the world I believe. There you can learn any language. It was right in the middle of Dresden. I met a few nice people and had fun.

I do not know why I picked English. Perhaps it was to understand Radio London, so I could hear what had been bombed lately. "There you heard it first," they said. And I was very interested in finding out how everything was at home, even though it was not permitted to listen to that channel.

One day I was caught at work by a medic from Austria. This fellow was ready to turn me in but our Stabsarzt Dr. Muller talked him out of it. That could have been very bad for me. Dr. Muller instructed me never to try it again.

When I think of it, Dr. Muller was so special in everything. I owe him so much. I am still trying to find him to thank him for all he had done for us. Who knows, he might still be alive.

Chapter 8
Dresden, while it died with 130,000 People

A telegram arrived for me from home. Our Theo was no more. How was that possible? It said he died in Hannover? What was he doing there? He was in Russia somewhere when I'd last heard from him. Mama said to come home right away. When I got home I was afraid that Mama had lost her mind. Charlott had to tell me the story.

Theo did come home unexpectedly for a few days. He and his buddy were elected to go home to deliver a package to an officer's wife, who lived in the area. It was good news for both, since they'd been away from home for a long time.

First, they went to his friend's house and found it destroyed by bombs and both parents killed. Neighbors had told them the story. It must have been a terrible shock for them but they had to go on.

Theo invited him to come and meet our mom and new stepfather. They were both sure to get a good meal and a couple of good nights' sleep. But it was not to be.

When they found Mama's new home, they rang the doorbell and instead of Mama, it was our new stepdad that opened the door.

What happened then was the meanest and most sickening part in my story, in fact of anything that I've ever heard. He was drunk and upset at the time and told both of the boys to leave. Mama came out, hugged her son and cried. Theo never expected a welcome like that. After a loud discussion, he agreed that Theo could stay, but not his friend. I cannot understand disliking that boy in uniform who came with my brother, that was family. He must have been completely drunk or out of his mind.

Theo left with his friend. What else could he do? It was not his home. He did not have one anymore. They found themselves a place to spend the night and met Mama the following morning. I could cry out loud every time I think about t. Mama took the last pictures of them in front of a church in Karlsruhe. It was the last picture taken.

Now they had to make their way back to the Russian front again. Later, I found out the rest of this sad story.

Thec and his friend boarded the train to return to the front. They met two girls from Hannover. I believe they had enough time together to talk about their big disappointments. The train came to a complete stop right in the middle of nowhere.

They were told to get out and away, since there were airplanes overhead. The city was not far from there. They started to walk after being invited to one of the girl's house. They met the parents and were invited to eat and stay until the next morning.

They must have been having a good time when there was another alarm and both her mother and father had to leave. It was their job to help the people on the street and see that all the lights were out. The parents told them to make sure to go to the cellar and left. The bombs started falling and every place was in turmoil. After it was all clear again and the parents came out from wherever they were, they found the big corner building of heavy stone gone.

After 24 hours of digging with heavy equipment, they found all four huddled together, dead.

Mama was notified that Theo's body was buried right away in Hannover Limmer.

She wanted to go to that cemetery right away but at that time it was impossible. I had to go back to Dresden, Charoltt was worried about taking Christa on the train, and Mama was absolutely not well enough. We decided to wait a few days and I promised to try to come back again soon.

After I left to go back to Dresden, Mama went to Karlsruhe to start divorce procedures. I found out later because of that, a brand new catastrophe had started.

Mama had gone to the first lawyer that she could find, broke down, and told him the whole story. She mentioned over and over that the boys would still be alive had her husband not treated them the way he had.

Mama said the man just sat there without saying anything, just listening until she had it all off of her chest and he looked very angry. Then he excused himself and went out of the room. When he came back, there was a man in uniform with him and she had to repeat everything again, which he wrote down. When she was through, he told her that he knew the man, that he was a troublemaker and that they'd had their eyes on him. When Mama told us that, we got worried. A uniformed man? He had no right to be there, but Mama didn't care. All she wanted was to be free of the man that was to blame for our Theo's death.

She should have known that this man in uniform could do her more harm than good. But at the time, she did not care. He was arrested after refusing to help after a bombing. He was taken to prison and later was shot for being a troublemaker.

We all knew that it was wrong. Nobody had the right to do that and I think we all agreed. However at the time, we were all hurt and full of grief. Nothing made sense anymore. Everything at that time was unfair and horrible.

I told Dr. Muller about the way things were and he made it possible for me to return to Bruschal. He'd met Mama once and liked her and he understood.

Back in Bruchsal, I found Mama confused and depressed but we had to get moving, and we did. First we had to store furniture and personal items in the basement she had rented. Hopefully they would be safe until she could get back. She was moving in with Mimi for a while. We had to pack. We had to see where our Theo was buried. That was a strange day. The sky was red and much darker. Somebody told us it was Karlsruhe, bombed and burning.

Mama had a lot of belongings there. We decided to go there first and see if anything was left. Everything was so mixed up. There was no other way. So we left. The whole neighborhood was still burning and not one fire truck in sight. The four-floor apartment house was burning. I tried to save something anyway. There was not much time so I just threw everything like bedding and clothes out of the window. Some of it was burned before it landed on the sidewalk below so we gave up. Just before I came down the stairs a beam fell behind me and I tripped on something and scooted down the stairs as if on a slide. I knew it was time to leave.

We sat in the train on the way to Hannover Limmer, where our Theo was laid to rest. We were both very tired and sad when I fell asleep in Mama's arms.

We found the parents of the girl that was with Theo. They had contacted Mama. They told us all about what had happened and showed us where they'd all died.

I had to take Mama away from there. On the way to the cemetery we had asked a lady on the street where the cemetery was located. She walked with us. She lived close by and invited us to come for coffee after we visited our Theo's grave. There were many new graves with temporary crosses of wood. Then we found him. His name on the wooden cross was proof he was right under our feet.

The kind lady invited us to spend the night and promised us to visit Theo's grave now and then. We wrote to each other for a long time and she always sent us new pictures. The last picture she sent us, showed a regular stone cross. She was a good person with many problems of her own. I don't know whatever happened to her.

Then we were on a train again. Mama was on her way back to Uckermunde to be with Mimi and her family and I, back to Dresden.

Everything was the same. I was back to doing what I had done before. I still lived in town except for one night a week when I had night duty. Still, we did not have many patients. Only a few beds were occupied with minor problems. It was one of those evenings when Dr. Muller reminded me not to forget to go to school. I told him about my night duty and after he checked rooms he said, "You can go to school, I made other arrangements here." It was the night when Dresden died, February 13, 1945.

I remember him saying, "Now make sure you go to school. Good night." And then buzzed off on his motorcycle.

I went to town. First bus, then streetcar, and walked the rest of the way home. My school was right in the middle of town but I had 2½ hours before class. I set my clock and had a little nap. It rang, but I did not feel like getting up and skipped school anyway. I'd never done that before.

Air raid. "Alarm." I jumped up. I'd never heard it in Dresden before. At first I did not want to go down to the shelter. However, after the bombs started to fall, I was on my way, and fast. We didn't want to think about it being our turn now. When the whole city burned, we had to believe it. The city kept burning, two days and three nights.

While waiting and finally an all clear, we all knew that our city was in big trouble. Looking out to see it, was horrible. Somebody said something about our roof burning and then there was another alarm. I just ran out to a few houses down the street to a different shelter. But, it had too many people in it already.

When the big bombs exploded, I truly believed that this would be the end. Bombs kept falling and falling. I was in a strange house and nobody would find me. I was thinking of Mama, Theo, and the rest of the family. All I had on was pajamas and a little sweater. I pushed myself in but it was only a laundry room in the cellar with an outside door.

Nobody knew me here. Heavy bombs fell everywhere and some so very close. Since Dresden was all lit up it was easy to finish the job.

Oh my God, what has happened to the human race I thought? I was huddled on the floor. We all expected to be killed. I just prayed to go quick. It seemed forever but the planes finally left. Slowly, we all went outside. The sky was bright red. I went back to the house. It was still there. We either had false information or somebody stopped the fire. I never asked. I just started walking with many people away from town. Nobody seemed to care if they were dressed or not. We just kept walking.

I knew we were pretty close to the train station. There were a few houses left on the edge of town. I made my way to the long country road, which led to the hospital where I worked.

I walked and walked for miles toward the little hospital or the hill. It was terrible. People were looking for help. Most of them were injured in the fire. Some were limping or crawling. Some even had body parts missing. One lady with a hand badly burned asked me to go back in the city to find her daughter. I knew that was impossible. It would have been suicide to try. I asked her to come with me. She was in terrific pain but she walked with me all the way.

When we came to the gate, I saw stretchers with dead and injured people all over the place. I saw my doctor. He looked like a butcher all covered with blood. He looked up when I called. I ran to him and he hugged me like I was one of his kids that were lost. It would have been hopeless to have gone to school that night. Now there was a lot to do and more help was on the way. I bandaged the burned with ointment that was black and smelled like tar, called Ichtiol.

We used all the barracks on the hill for those people. The stench of burnt flesh was unbearable, especially when you first arrived. Many soldiers from the school were called to help.

At first there was total chaos until everybody was assigned what to do and everything under control. All the patients were sent to hospitals far away and there they received proper care. After we had everything cleaned up and back in order, it was hard to see what had happened and for us it was unforgettable. We were not to go to town for a while, so we all lived in the barracks again.

I was thinking about Gunther's mom, who lived near the heart of the city on the hill called, "Weise Hirsch." I just had to go. I had promised to check on her. I went on foot of course, even though we were warned not to go there since there were still delayed bombs going off. I had to walk right through town. I passed horrible sights close to where the railroad station used to be. When I reached what used to be Dresden, it was just as this picture shows.

I had to walk over and around bodies, which had to be gathered and burned. Neighbors told me Gunther's mother had also lost her home and had moved. They told me where to find her. We were glad to know that we both were still alive. I helped her save a few things that were left in her old cellar. We moved her belongings in a little wagon to her new home.

We all knew that the war was as good as over, but nobody dared to say it out loud. We were told that we could not surrender and it would be terrible the things that could happen to us. We were especially warned about the Russians, who were getting closer and closer. We had been given orders that Dresden was to be defended.

Unexpectedly, we were ordered closer to town, to a very large hospital. It had been used for mental patients.

We all were worried. We were just a very small group, maybe ten or twelve all together in this big empty stone building. We had only one doctor and no medicine. What were we to do there? There was nothing for us to do except wait.

According to David Irvings well-known book, "The Destruction of Dresden," one hundred and thirty five thousand people died on February the thirteenth, 1945.

Chapter 9
Radio Announcement "Hitler Dead"

Dr. Muller left one day and came back with food. Things we had not seen in years. There were whole hams, bread, sugar, coffee, and liquor. We must have had our mouths wide open, while we watched him putting it all on a table. When the cases were empty, he divided the treasures among all of us there. While he did that, he explained what had happened. Someone, an officer I believe told Dr. Muller about a boat in the Elbe River loaded with food that could not be moved. He had permission to take what he could before the Russians took it over.

I can still see all of us around a very large dining room table on the third floor eating like kings when the news that Hitler was dead was announced on the radio. We all looked at Dr. Muller who was sitting at the end of the table. He did not get up, not even after they played our national anthem. He just kept on eating. Nobody said anything until it was all over. We all were waiting to hear what he had to say.

Then very calmly, he said, "Finally, now listen up everybody go right away. Find your family. Be careful and fast."

Then he turned to a medic, who was not from that part of the country and said, "You come with me to where I am going, but first let us get some more of that food from the boat anchored in the river."

Then he turned around to me and said, "And you wait right here, and don't move. We will pick you up very soon since you are better off here then where we are going."

They went to the ambulance and he called and said to all, "God be with you and good luck."

A little later I was alone. Oh, how I wished that they had taken me. Right then I had to trust them to come back for me. Very worried, I stood by the street praying that everything would be all right.

I waited a long time by the street and noticed that something was going on. Many people were running, pushing carts and little wagons, all going in the same direction. I called to find out just what was going on but nobody seemed to hear me.

Then I heard somebody say that they were very close. I then knew what they were talking about. The murdering Russians were on their way in. For a few moments, I did not know what to do when I heard heavy guns in the distance. I had to decide right then but I lost control of myself. No way could I wait any longer. I grabbed somebody's bike that was leaning against the empty building and started running with the bike. I kept running with the rest of the people without the slightest idea where we were running to for some time.

Since nobody answered my question and I was so tired of running, I suddenly did not care anymore. It was all over anyway. I pushed the bike away from me and sat down. I think it was a big rock by the road. After I realized what I had done, I cried.

It must have been something like a hysterical breakdown. I did not care how I looked or sounded. All this had to have an end sometime.

Chapter 10
Russian Invasion

A lady dressed in black came over to me and asked me where I was going. After I told her, she reached for my hand and pulled me up. Then she saw the bike, which was not really mine. She picked it up and said something like, "come quick, there is no time to waste, we can talk later." We must have walked about two more miles and then she pointed to the right. There I saw a little village in the valley. "I live down there," she said. "This road will take you all the way to Prag." "Of course! I read a sign a ways back that said Prager Strasse." It was just the opposite way for me to go home.

On the way down the hill she introduced herself as Frau Handra and told me that she had just lost her husband. I told her my name and a little about myself.   She also mentioned that there were already two ladies in her house. A mother and daughter from Estland, "And that is good" she said, because both speak the Russian language.

I felt better, but not good, since I knew there had to be a lot of trouble to come. I just felt it.

After I met the girls, whose names I forget, we ate some of the good food I had tied to the bike and talked. While we were sitting at the table, a neighbor told us all to come and see the Burgermeister. He wanted to talk to us right now.

He was an older man. I respected him right away. He told us all to go home and hang white bed sheets out of the windows. We were also instructed to find bells, whistles, or any other noisemakers to use if we needed help.   He expected these Russian soldiers to come to our village after dark. So if anybody was in trouble, we should make a lot of noise. All neighbors should go there together to help us (help us?). That did not make much sense at the time but we were ready (for what?).

We all did what he said. The whole village had bed sheets hanging out of the windows. We were now looking behind the curtains way up the hill. Waiting!

They came! We saw them coming one after the other in wooden wagons pulled by horses. Trucks, olive drab with white stars, filled with soldiers.

I found out later that those were American trucks driven by Russians. We talked about what we would do next and decided that the two girls from Estland, who spoke Russian, would answer the door. Slowly they came down towards the village. I could not stand it any longer. I went upstairs and hid behind the bed. There was just enough room for me since the wall up there was slanted and I was glad it did. It seemed that someone had said, "Now!" All at once there were terrible noises, like hell broke loose.

Bells rang and pots and pans were banged together. There was yelling. Animals and chickens were butchered. It was unbelievable. Our front door was kicked in and there the Russians stood with guns in hand. Twice, one of them came upstairs, looked around and left. There were big fires outside now and singing and dancing to their everlasting rhythm.

They gathered all the girls with their guns in one hand and the Vodka bottle in the other. Even the old ladies were not spared.

So that is what it has come to, and most likely, will it be like that from now on?

The next morning Frau Handra called me to come downstairs and said, "I understand that you are afraid, but remember you cannot live up there all the time, you have to realize that they can do what they want now and will stay in our land from now on."

Many incredible things happened. I am afraid to say more. I did not listen anymore. There was no way I would live like that There had to be a way to get out.

Mrs. H. told me what I could do to get away. She told me to get up very early, while they were still asleep, take off my shoes and very quietly come down the stairs, then get outside, run up the hill to the small little train station. A train would stop there every morning headed for Dresden. I should get on it anyway I could. There was a restroom where I could hide until the train arrived.

I did exactly what she said. Thanked her for everything and went out to the street. But to my horrible surprise, I saw those little panja wagons with horses all along the street and Russian soldiers were sleeping under them.

I could not go back in the house, since Mrs. H. had gone in and closed the door.

With shoes in hand and a few other things, I ran passed all those wagons and trucks until I reached the station.

The train was standing at the station. All empty boxcars, I believe, at least the one I climbed in was. My heart pounded very hard. That was a miracle for sure and I thanked God. To this day, I cannot believe I got away. How and when I jumped off, I just don't recall. I finally ended up at my boyfriend Gunther's home. His mother told me that I could live with her and not to worry since nobody ever bothered them in town.

She was right. No Russian soldiers ever came to the house. I was thankful. Gunther would be coming home somehow and I hoped that there would be some kind of order again soon.

I helped Gunther's mother as much as I could. I went with the wagon all the way to her old bombed house and got everything that was left. She was not a lady that was easy to please or to love but I did not feel I was a burden to her. . I could not help being very homesick.

We never had enough food to eat. A good friend of hers, a hotel owner, gave me a job in their kitchen. Russian soldiers lived there. They paid me with food for the work I did. At first I did not want to go to work there, but I went, and it was not bad at all. As I recall, all I did was peel potatoes. These Russian soldiers looked different. They were taller and their uniforms were cleaner looking.

My hometown, Baden-Baden was ruled by the French troops. Could we all go to Luxembourg maybe? Would they take us in? What happened to my homeland? Every other nation has a piece of it so what are we now, and what did I do to deserve this treatment? I had a lot of thinking to do while I was working. I always had help at home, now everything was up to me. Heaven help me. I just had to go home.

I wanted to go home so badly. While I peeled all those potatoes, I wondered how I could travel back home. I thought surely they must be worried about me. I wondered how the American soldiers behaved. I was told it was much better there, but how did they know?

One evening after work, I found a note at the front door. It was an order for me to go to a certain place to work. I believe it was some kind of factory. I remember a few freight cars, which had to be filled with horseshoes. There were big piles of them, four in a bundle, wired together. They had to be loaded fast. It was the first time I saw Russian girls in uniform. They were speaking poorly in German but kept saying, "Mach schnell oder arbeiten die ganze nacht." It meant, "Hurry up or you will work all night."

I wished that I had some gloves because the wires were sticking out and we had to throw them to each other all the way to the boxcar. We just could not do all the work before dark and were told to come back the next morning.

I saw a lot of those boxcars and it looked like people were living in them. The sliding doors were open and we could see inside. The floors were layered with carpets. There was valuable furniture stacked inside. Chandeliers were hung in there, all ready to be shipped to Russia, I believe.

That evening, on the way home, I saw a Russian soldier and a Russian girl in uniform walking toward me on the same sidewalk. I knew that they would stop me, so I crossed over to the other side of the street. They did the same and stopped me. Neither one could speak German but the girl motioned to my jacket. I took it off and gave it to her. Then she pointed to my skirt and blouse. They both laughed and kept on walking.

When I got to the apartment, I needed a kind word very badly, but Mrs. W. smiled after I'd told her what had just happened and said something like, "And so? There is nothing you can do about it."

All at once, I did not like her anymore. She was not what I thought she was. No compassion, no hug, or a kind word. And even the thought that she was my boyfriend's mother did not matter. I needed to leave real soon and didn't even care to see Gunther again. His mom was a schoolteacher, his dad was killed, but not in the war, it was some kind of hunting accident. Gunther was all she had and not at all interested in me. Right there, I made plans.

I needed to go home where I was loved and wanted. But at the time, there was no chance for that. Dorle, my friend came. She knew about Gunther's mom and found me. I had not seen her for a long time. It was a happy surprise to see her again.

Dorle told me that she was leaving Dresden to try the now English Zone of Germany. People were better treated there she said. Right away, I decided to go part way with her.

But then I remembered, Dr. Muller. He had told me when we parted, that he would take me where his family was located in Rhaten by Dresden, on top of tall cliffs. I heard him talk about that place many times. His sister-in-law owned a little restaurant for mountain climber's way up on top of those cliffs.

I found them after a long, steep walk. Somebody who knew the family walked with me. They were all there on top of the world.

The wind was very strong up there and the restaurant very small, but cozy.

The medic from the hospital where I had worked, whose name I do not remember, also lived with them. It was he that showed me a little cave where they kept the food.

They had the strangest outhouse I had ever seen. It was built on two close cliffs. It looked like an outhouse from the outside but when you looked down the hole in the seat, you got dizzy. It was a long way down. I never used it.

When Dr. Muller came, we had a good dinner and a bottle of wine. I told them my story and they told me theirs. If I had only waited a few more minutes longer the day I ran with the bicycle, I would've been away from it all, way up here. But now, I had to go home. We were singing (just imagine), singing out loud since we were halfway to heaven and nobody could hear us.

They never had an unwanted visitor up there. Not yet anyway. I left them, feeling so much better. I traveled back to Mrs. W., told her that I had made up my mind to go home. I also explained where I had been and showed her the nice letter of recommendation that our Stabersarzt Dr. Muller had given me.

I still have it. It is all yellow from age and one of very few things I have left.

Chapter 11
The Long Way Home on Foot

I was ready to go home. All 1,000 kilometers on foot if it came to that. I met an Army nurse also headed west. We were instant friends and both determined to get home. She had heard of a place where people gathered to go over to the American zone. It was in a woody area. We both decided to mingle and find out how to go about it.

There were two German soldiers on their way home. We heard their conversation about the American zone. We begged them to take the two of us along until we are out of the Russian zone. They did not like the idea of being bothered with two strange women. They told us not to misunderstand them. In normal times they would gladly help us, but they could not risk it. We would be either too noisy or lag behind. In other words, they did not want the responsibility. It was forbidden to cross. We begged them and promised not to be in their way. We left them no choice, so they allowed us to come along.

We started out not even knowing each other's name. It was way after dark when we passed a little Russian guardhouse with about twenty or more people. Everybody was quiet as a mouse. I knew there was at least one small child in the bunch but not a sound was made. We passed and disappeared into "no-mans-land." Then walked about five more miles until we saw a tent with American soldiers and a number of people like us, going nowhere.

It so happened that the Americans were not allowed to let us cross the line. The four of us watched them from a distance. They served old people coffee and gave doughnuts to the children.

We were on the edge of a dense forest beside a street or road, which was guarded by two American soldiers. We noticed right away how clean they were, with polished helmets, yellow scarves, and pressed pants. What a difference it was between them and the Russians. Russian uniforms looked like leather from all the dirt and grease on them. They smelled bad and their faces were full of pockmarks. They were also very short. We figured that they might have come from Mongolia.

These American soldiers were actually friendly, but we trusted nobody.

The boys scouted around. They told us that the two American soldiers on the street carried their rifles upright. Once in awhile, they shot them up in the air after somebody crossed the road to freedom.

We had to get to the other side of the road, since the Russian soldiers could come any time to chase us back again. We sat in the bushes for a while, and then one of the boys crossed the road. Nothing happened. Then his friend crossed. Nothing again. Now the nurse followed. I was right behind her when we heard a shot and I did a stupid thing. Instead of running the rest of the way, I ran back and was the only one left on the wrong side!

Now all three over there tried to talk me into crossing. I was so afraid now that they had seen us. I was sure they'd shoot me.

Then one of the boys said, "Well if you want to stay, then stay, we're on our way. We told you." That did it. I ran across and without a word kept on running. We all ran until we could not run anymore. Finally we felt safe.

We knew that if they wanted us back, it would have been very easy to get us and they knew that we were there and let us go anyway.

When we sat down for the first time and looked at each other, we all laughed and introduced ourselves.

I only remember one was named "Slim". I don't remember what they looked like exactly but I do remember them being nice looking and in a hurry to go home. Just like us. The soldier who seemed to be in charge was much bigger and stronger than Slim. He said that Slim played the organ like an angel.

After we had asked a farmer for something to eat, we met a priest in a little chapel and asked if Slim could play the organ. I don't know about the others, but I had the feeling that we all prayed and thanked God. They were truly two beautiful people.

Now we slept in barns and fields wherever we could but never a bed, until we got home. The more people we saw, the less chance we had to get something to eat.

The farmers could not help us anymore since there were too many people seeking help. But they all wished us good luck and a safe trip home.

We found a train station. It was packed with people, mostly German soldiers on their way home. They were hanging on to the doors and windows and sitting on top of the train. People even sat on the coal car behind the locomotive. We found a place up there too.

When we were just about to leave, an American soldier climbed up. He did not do or say anything, just acted like he was one of us and wiggled his way between us to sit down.

After a while, he went through his bag and took out a can of pork and beans. Everybody watched him. It was very embarrassing, but I did too. Then he poked a hole in the can and lit up some kind of stick with which he heated the can. Then something more embarrassing happened. When he was ready to eat his beans, he looked at us and noticed that everybody was watching him. Most of us looked away now, but it was too late. He stood up and passed the can around. Nobody said, "No thank you." We all had between two and five beans.

We were all glad to have met him. He started talking with the people next to him. We went through a small, but dirty, tunnel and came out dirty on the other side. We all laughed together.

Soon after the train ride, the boys left us. We decided to stay on the Autobahn. Walking was easier plus we hoped to get a ride from somebody.

There were no German people on the road. We saw many Jeeps and trucks but no civilian cars. We kept walking; sooner or later we would be home.

Ther a big American truck stopped. The driver pointed for us to climb in. We just about did until the canvas opened in back and we saw that it was packed with American soldiers.

We were not ready for that even though our feet hurt. The next thing we did was stupid. We turned around and walked back the way we came until they drove away.

After a long time, another truck stopped. It was smaller, open, and had a bench on each side. We rode there and in no time at all we saw a sign that said Bruchsal. I got off and my new friend went on. I thanked the driver, they said, "okay." Finally I was on familiar ground.

There was still about an hour to walk, but I was so light-hearted because I was just about home.

When I came close to town I saw with horror, that Bruchsal had been bombed. I was now standing where the train station used to be.

I sat down and fell apart again, and again somebody, a real old lady, saw me. After I told her where I lived she said, "I better go with you." I thought for sure that my people were gone but our house was still there. There were a few people standing across the street.

Somebody called my name from a window across the street. It was a neighbor that recognized me. She said not to worry and that everybody was still alive. Also, that my sister

Charlott and little Christa had just left the house and had entered the park. I saw them and called out. They turned around and we fell into each other's arms, filled with happiness.

Chapter 12
Home at Last

I was home again but new problems came up. When I applied for my ration card, I was told that there was no room for me in Bruchsal. The city was so badly bombed and too many people needed a home. They told me to go back to where I came from or try to find a place somewhere else. I felt like somebody had punctured my balloon. Stunned and down in the dumps again I explained that this was my hometown and that I was sent away. Also, that I came more or less, by foot all the way from Dresden (1,000 km). I told them I was living with my sister. They then showed me a book, a waiting list for people that had lost their homes and said, "If there is room for more at your sister's place, we will send somebody there. That means the next one in this book."

It was like the whole world was going mad all over again. I ended up breaking the rules again and stayed with Charlott and Heinz anyway, but without ration cards. I was not as undernourished as they were, but hungry like them just the same.

After a while, I decided to go to Baden-Baden, which was occupied by French troops. I visited my friends there and heard of a place, a group of black marketers.

I went and found out that all I had to do was deliver food to different people. Of course, if I would have been caught, I don't know what would have happened to me. As soon as I managed to get a few items like bread, flour, margarine, and sugar (in very small quantities), I went back home to Bruschal to share my treasure.

I never told my family exactly how involved it was at times. This went on for some time. I visited the ration office many times. You could depend on your luck just so much. I was not a gambler.

By this time, they knew me at the rations office, but the answer was pretty much the same. What in the world did they think I lived on?

At that time, jobs were hard to find, but there was always school someone said and also farmers needed help in the fields. If I would do both and proved it, I could get permission to stay, since I was already at my sister's.

They gave me the address of a potato farmer. The next morning I was on my way. It was a long way out of town on foot, but working there, I would be legal to live at home. What is the world coming to! I thought.

I kept on walking and thinking that all this would soon pass and maybe for the better, when I heard somebody call my name. It was Heinz, my brother-in-law, on his bike. He came to take me back home. He said, "Charlott and I decided that there must be another way. Let's go home. We will talk about it." I got on the back of the bike and went back home. That was so sweet of them.

I ended up working for the potato farmer. Actually, gathering potatoes was not that bad. I did not mind the work, but it seemed that the new rules were no better than the old ones.

70

I went to Berlitz School again in Karlsruhe and received my ration card. Now I was legal again.

Ever so slowly, things got better. Charlott and I sewed up a storm. We made ourselves new wardrobes. It is surprising what you can do if you are determined. I made hats, copies from the new magazines, and even shoes with straw soles just like the Italians made. I found some moss green canvas and they were beautiful. Everybody wanted me to make some for them. I had no time for that except for the real old lady below us. She had asked me and I just couldn't say no to her since she was so nice.

I went for walks in the forest a lot. Never before had I walked that far and I wondered later on why I was there.

I found an apple tree, where an apple tree had no business being. It was sort of like a wonder. There were no houses in sight. The tree was loaded with yellow apples. The apples were ripe, not so big, but very good. I grabbed a few and walked home fast, well I guess I ran home fast, to tell Heinz and Charlott. It was a good size tree. We went right away with sacks and a little wagon, with Christa on top.

They were surprised. We picked two sacks of apples and the tree didn't look touched. What fun we had.

We cooked some for applesauce; we baked some and dried the rest in rings on long strings across the windows. Other then being invaded by yellow jackets, it was great. We sewed little sacks of cloth to store the rest.

On one of our sewing days, we were talking about Mama's sewing machine. One of the old peddle machines that was stored in somebody's cellar before it was bombed. We knew about it, but had never gone there, so we went looking. We didn't think we'd find anything from what it looked like. Also, by now we were tougher and could take the disappointment.

Somebody else must have been there on one end of the place. Someone had started to dig enough to crawl in to check. With our spades in hand we poked, dug, and scraped but all we could see was evidence that everything was burned and broken. After awhile, we found all kinds of pieces of furniture. We still couldn't help it and cried a lot every time we uncovered another of Mama's treasures. Charlott uncovered our big set of china. Everything from coffee cups, teacups, platters, round and oval bowls, candleholders, pepper and salt shakers, everything in pieces. Mama called it zwiebel muster "onion set" blue and white. The old fashioned type. We had only used it for very special days like Christmas. There were other memories such as the old grandfather clock, the old gramophone, buffet, etc. All of it was destroyed.

We were about to leave when we saw part of the sewing machine in the rubble. We dug it up. Of course all the wooden parts were burned off and the machine itself was all twisted up.

I remember it was beautiful ironwork that I had to dust in my childhood and hated to do that.

Mama did not even know that she had lost the whole household. She was still in Pommern and we hadn't gotten any mail from her for a long time.

Chapter 13
"The Visitor" (New Problems in Store)

While I was in Baden-Baden, Charlott had a visitor one morning. He was not in any kind of uniform, nor did he show any identification, but was very demanding and nasty. Heinz was at work at the time. He wanted to know where my mother was. Charlott was at first confused and then angry. He said that Mama was to blame that Mr. S., Mama's ex-husband, was killed and they were looking for her. Charlott wanted to know who he was but he would not say. Charlott told him to leave even though she was afraid of him and alone in the house. That was gutsy of her, not at all like her.

After I came home, we tried to figure out what to do. Had we not gone through enough? What was all that about? How much more could Mama take after what she went through? Theo meant so much to her and he had been turned away from home. How could she have possibly lived with a man like him? She had to divorce him.

First, Charoltt wanted to go to the public authority in Karlsruhe but we decided it was not the right time for that, since we had no proper law just yet and decisions were many times made in haste.

We wrote a letter to Mama. There was always a small chance that she would get it. We told her to stay where she was, until we knew what was going on. But when she received the letter she decided to come right home anyway. It was an incredible journey, but she made her way to Heidelberg. We went to get her and hardly recognized her. It was at night when we arrived there. She told us about her trip. It must have been like a nightmare. She never knew what was coming up next. (I know, I write all that in details but I don't think we were alone to have so much misery).

Mama came home all alone, and was barely able to hear anymore. We had to decide what to do. Mama wanted to go to the authorities also, but Charlott had a better idea. She found out where the displaced people gathered to be shipped home to their country and found a group from Luxembourg She made friends right away and Mama was checked in, to stay until all papers were in order to leave. Here they all lived in barracks, which were clean and warm. They were well fed and very happy.

Afterwards, Charlott came home and told us that Mama was safe. She then decided to go to Karlsruhe to the authority and demanded to be informed of what was going on. She was told that no such person was ordered or justified to visit us. They knew about Mr. S., that he was shot, but assured her that it had nothing to do with Mama's divorce. That was the end of our problems.

Mama was happy in Luxembourg with all her brothers and sisters. We could not visit her there. This little country was tighter than a drum. I wished every country could be like that. Everybody should mind their own business, stay independent, and keep their boys safe.

As a seventy-five year old great grandma talking, think about that. Luxembourg must have done something right, to never be involved. Mama should have known better and stayed there in the first place. That is what I meant in the beginning of this book when I said, "She was not as wise as she was pretty."

Chapter 14
Waiting and Hoping

I visited Baden-Baden whenever I could. Most of my friends lived there but the last time I must have left my identity card (ken card) there, as it was lost. I knew I had to go back to get it, since we were ordered to carry it with us at all times. Nobody had ever asked me for it, so I wasn't worried too much.

In 1946, there were many American soldiers, but we had no problem with them. They left us alone and if they did not, they were punished under their law.

One morning, we saw them marching by the house. Charlott had called me to the window, "You have to see this," she said.

They were so relaxed and not at all concerned or listening to their sergeant trying to keep them in step. Nobody listened to what he said.

Some were smoking and some walking in groups apart, laughing and kicking a can.

Some chewed gum and had a good time just clowning around. It was actually comical and different now that the war was over. It was good for us to see that. They were humans and not the monsters we were made to believe. Why did we not trust them? More and more they blended in like they belonged there.

We were waiting for our soldiers to come home. They were scattered all over the world. Slowly, they did return. It was heart breaking at times, the way they looked. Once so proud and now after they had given their all, beaten and tired. And worst of all, they were hated all over the world. Why?

After awhile, that changed too. Everybody went to work. There were no lazy people. I never saw a bum on the streets at home while I was there. Everybody had plenty to do and soon there was a lesson learned and a reason to live again.

More and more came home, but of course, not our Theo. He was so determined to stay alive and assured us that he'd be able to survive. I remember when he was home and we talked about which food we would eat first once the war was over.

When it was Theo's turn, he said, "When this stinking war is over, I will make myself a sandwich with this much butter on it." With his fingers he showed us about one inch. I don't think his wish was ever granted while he was alive, but he was truly a good person and I believed in God.

Heinz, my brother-in-law, had a lot of irons in the fire. At first, he worked for the Bruchsal newspaper and was soon well known for his articles and cartoon-like drawings. They were mostly on the funny side, which was very much needed at the time. His first love was still to become an architect. He was able to achieve his dream much later. I have a large collection of his work and look at it now and then. What wonderful memories. We were so proud of him.

Heinz was wounded three times in Russia. Once in each hand and once in his side. He can still do anything, except play his violin.

Heinz

Chapter 15
Met my Partner for Life and the Long Trip to the USA

One morning in spring 1946, I was elected to go to the milkman. It was not far and I didn't mind. The weather was beautiful and the sun was out and it felt pretty good. I decided to take the longer way through the park. The castle was still sad to look at and there were wildflowers between the rubble of war.

On the way back, I sat down on an old park bench in the sun. Everything was so nice, warm, and peaceful. I poured myself a bit of milk in the lid of the can to drink, when I saw an American Jeep with two military police. They were driving slowly through the middle of the park. The bench I sat on was just parallel and I was glad. I remembered what they looked like while they passed. The driver was a big fellow that looked very stern, maybe even mean. The other one was small and very boy-like with freckles and red hair. Both wore helmets and yellow scarves and wooden sticks at their sides. I did not see a gun. I was lucky this time and I made up my mind to go to Baden-

Baden to get my pass. Then I saw them turn their Jeep into the walkway where I sat. They were coming back. I poured the milk I was about to drink back in the container when they stopped. The big one wanted to see my Ken card (my I.D.).

What could I say? It was such a long story so I pretended that I did not understand what he was saying and after he replied with the word "ken card," which is German for I.D. I told them in English that I left it at home and that I lived close by, hoping that was good enough.

They talked about it and decided to go home with me to get it. Now I had to come clean. I told them my story and promised to take care of it. They must have known that I was telling the truth but enjoyed the way I was so scared of what might happen. They had a conversation in a very low voice so I could not understand. I noticed that they were having fun with me. They had no intention of arresting me, but did not let me in on that yet.

They decided that they would give me time to get my I.D. and invited me to a baseball game the following weekend. I had never heard of baseball. It was not played in Germany. I did not hear which one I was to meet and I did not ask or care. I was sure I would not be there.

I came home and told Charlott. She laughed and said something like, "Don't worry about it but get that ken card right away." I had that meeting on my mind all the way to Baden-Baden on the train and I hoped to get my I.D. back.

I was pretty sure that it was the big guy I was to meet. With my retrieved ken card in my purse, I would look him straight in the eye and mention that I was not afraid of him. I even hoped for an apology for making me feel like a child, afraid of the big bad wolf. Now that I had that dumb pass, I would make sure he knew he didn't scare me.

The morning I was to meet whomever, I asked Christa to be my little spy. I needed to find out who was in the park waiting for me. She soon came back and reported that there was a big American (in an Army uniform) sitting on the wooden fence by the pond.

I had mixed feelings about the whole thing but decided to go anyway. Yes, it was the big mean one, but he did not look so tough to me now, with no helmet or stick. He smiled, jumped off the fence, and we started walking and talking. I don't remember going to any ballgame.

He saw my I.D. card and then he knew my name. He told me his and that he'd come from Chicago. I also found out that his mom and dad's ancestors came from Germany about three generations back.

So, he was Clarence Joseph Burger, a German name in fact, more German than I was, since my Mama came from Luxembourg. He never corrected my still bad English. I guess he did not care. We understood each other and at the end of that day we decided to see each other again.

CJ was stationed in Bruchsal for a few months and then moved to Karlsruhe. From there he came to see us regularly.

In the meantime, Heinz was rebuilding a just about totaled house. He was promised a nice little apartment after it was rebuilt. It had more rooms, but I missed the old place. Heinz could build the new apartment the way he wanted and that was important to him.

The friendship between CJ and I was growing, when I had an unexpected visitor. It was Gunther. He had been taken prisoner somewhere in Italy and held in a P.O.W. camp. Now on his way home and he came to see me first. He had in mind to take me back to the Russian zone. I don't think he knew all about his beloved Dresden. I didn't really have to think about that. Never, would I go back there again. We didn't know each other well enough since we had hardly seen each other in years. We thought we were in love once, but only in letters.

I was very sure I did not want to live with his mother again. I did not tell him that. I also never told him about my American friend. At the time, I did not think I should. Had I loved him enough, I would have or most likely asked him to stay in West Germany. Gunther left. I think he understood. We said goodbye and wished each other good luck and promised to keep in touch.

CJ was a quiet fellow and did not talk much. I did, and he just listened. When he decided to talk, he was honest and dependable. I could tell.

He did not like to go where people were dancing. That was a little hard for me since music was in my blood and there was music everywhere.

Dancing was not proper during the war. Most boys were fighting and too much misery was in the land. It was not forbidden exactly, but when you think about it, there was no time to celebrate. But with the war over it was high time to come alive.

We never went to hear a concert, opera, or theatre together. Once in awhile though, we saw an American movie and went for long drives through the country. I must say, I saw more of Germany than ever before.

One time when we went to see a movie, CJ waited until we were well into the story when he started holding my hand, and to my surprise he placed a ring on my finger. I didn't know what to think! I thought at first it was just a friendship ring. Later, we decided to get married.

My landlady and her husband gave us a very nice engagement party. Heinz, Charlott, and Christa came from Bruchal and most of our friends were there.

Getting married at that time was a little more than complicated but we were not in a big hurry just yet.

We planned on a simple, but beautiful church wedding with lots of flowers, a pretty gown, and lots of pictures for the memory box. After all, it would be the end of the first part of our lives and the beginning of the rest of our lives for which "we" were in charge.

After we found out there was a baby on the way, there was no time to lose. We started filling out form after form and waited. By the time we had permission and were legal, I was as big as a house (a big house) and we decided to wait.

Our baby was born and he was beautiful, healthy, and good as gold. Everything was just fine now. We planned our church wedding but CJ had orders to go back to the States. Now we had just a few days to get married. We went first to the Burgermeister, who was out for lunch and took his time to get back to the office. Finally, we were married.

I wonder sometimes if CJ understood everything that was said, but he did say, "ya" to make it legal. Then he rushed me home, since he had to travel back to camp to do whatever he had to, to get ready.

I was home with Charlott and couldn't believe what had just happened. My ring was now on the other hand and there was a big beautiful wedding cake waiting for us. She had used all our rations of eggs, sugar, and flour for a whole month. We had waited so long for the Burgermiester, and my husband didn't even have time to have a piece of cake until the next day. "This is the American way," Charlott said and laughed.

Little Mike was asleep and couldn't care less about all the fussing. Charlott fell in love with our little boy and had the nerve to ask me to leave him with her until I was settled somewhere in the United States.

Now I had a lot to do. We only had one day and anything that needed to be shipped had to be ready to go, since the Army would be picking it up.

We were ready now and waited for CJ's friend, an American from the camp. He offered to help us sell the car and take us to the plane. When he arrived he told us not to worry about our little Volkswagen. He assured us that we could trust him (but we never heard from him ever again) or of our little Bug.

I had never traveled in an airplane before and had never been close enough to see how big some of them were. Ours had four propellers and CJ assured me that they were very safe.

After we started to taxi, much to our surprise we were told that there was a problem. Something minor needed to be fixed. After a few hours we tried again. This time it was decided that we had to wait for the next day, something else was wrong. That was a bit scary for me.

The next morning, everything was ready. I was not frightened anymore.

PART TWO

USA
1948 - 2000

Chapter 16
Arrival in the USA and New Experiences

There were many people on this plane. We had nice seats by the window and since our baby was so little, they installed a small bed for him right in front of me. I remember how good I felt looking at him. He was comfortable in there and never out of sight.

The diaper supply was low by now and I asked, "What happens if we run out of them?" There was no way to wash them. CJ laughed and said, "We can always wrap him up in my underwear. Don't worry so much. We will get there soon. Take a nap while you can." No way, I thought.

We talked a little about Chicago. I had heard so much about that city of gangsters. He assured me that was all talk and that I would love his parents and like Chicago.

We had to land in Newfoundland. Neither of us can remember why, but we waited there. It was very cold just before Christmas in 1948. I was worried since things did not go exactly the way we were told. We had the diaper situation plus baby Mike was on a special formula, which I was supposed to prepare. We boarded the warm plane again and everything was all right.

We had decided to stop in a hotel long enough to get cleaned up, rest a little, and of course, take care of the diaper problem. The trip was so much longer then we expected.

When we finally arrived in Chicago, there was no more talk about a hotel. My husband decided to go straight home. "They are waiting," he said, "and we have a washer and dryer in the basement and you can soak in the tub." That sounded real good.

Oh joy! When our taxi stopped in front of the Burger residence, we noticed right away all the cars parked in front of the house. Through the windows we saw there were many people waiting for us.

I was not ready for that. I wished I could have disappeared into that basement with my son.

Ma, my mother-in-law, took little Mikey. (He had enough sleep and for him it was morning time and he did let us know that.) That did not help. She went right to the bedroom and changed him before I could say anything. Here was little Mikey in his Papa's olive green underwear, size large. That was not the best moment in my life.

It was Christmastime and CJ had to report to Fort Lee, VA right after the holidays. I had to stay in Chicago while he was looking for a home for us. Actually, I do not remember anything about that Christmas. It came and went and was bitter cold in Chicago, but the house was overheated.

Everybody was very good to me. There was Ma and Pa, Grandma Reuter, and Hank. He had lived with the family since he came to the USA from Germany as a young man. I remember many evenings we all sat down in the big basement. We all sang to some old German records while the diapers were in the machines being washed and dried. Everybody liked Mike, and Ma was the best cook. When everybody came home in the evening, we always had a good time. But Pa, I liked best. I always waited for him to come home. He never said much, but there was something so peaceful and nice about him. I loved that man like a father. I will never forget him.

Nevertheless, I wanted to play house on my own and was happy when CJ called and said that he was coming to get us. He also had a little bad news. He said to find a decent apartment was just about impossible there at the time. The place he found was pretty bad but he would look around for something better right away.

It was about a month after our arrival in Chicago, when we moved to Petersburg, Virginia. I could see now what the problem was. The only place available was in a schoolhouse, which was to be condemned. Since there was such a shortage of homes for the soldiers with families stationed there, it was used for temporary quarters.

We went upstairs and found our three rooms in a row with a big padlock on each door. It was not very inviting to say the least. Now we knew why the lady in charge told us that she would give us paint, "to kill the germs" (so help me Hanna) that is exactly what she had said. First we looked at each other. We had to take it there was no other choice. With a lot of soap, Ajax, and water, we both cleaned it up.

Now it didn't look so bad anymore. The windows were not blind like before and next I put up some curtains. What we didn't know was that we had roaches, lots of them – we only stayed here a short time.

Later we were transferred to Tacoma, Washington. We were very excited to say the least. We heard about the state located in the western corner of the United States and that it was called, "The Evergreen State." With forests even more beautiful then our beloved Black Forest in Germany and a heck of a lot larger. The more I read, the more I longed to live there with my family. We were actually ordered to go there, across the United States.

It was the longest, most beautiful train ride I'd ever had. We traveled through farmland, mountains, and deserts.

In the morning, we rushed to see more of America. We traveled through long dark tunnels, high bridges next to deep blue lakes, and rivers everywhere. I recall a real cowboy waving back to us. It was very easy to imagine how the first settlers felt. Since we were going to our "Promised Land," which it was to be, but not right away.

In 1949 we arrived in Tacoma, Washington. We walked out of the station and called a taxi to take us the rest of the way to Fort Lewis. That was a very busy place at that time.

And the first thing we heard was "No Quarters Available." They were all filled. Private housing was very scarce. Our name was put on a very long list. We were offered to live in a guesthouse for a week. That was nice, but with a little baby that wanted to cry once in awhile, was not so good since the walls were very thin.

It was a long week and we were without transportation so I walked up and down the long hall there with my baby. There I saw a board with all kinds of notes. Such as things for sale, places to go, and help wanted.

We were desperate. I read that several officers were looking for a maid. I did not like that word, but it said room and bath plus $20 a month.

I was never a maid before, but I knew how to do housework and take care of children. Oh boy! CJ did not like that at all, but something had to happen soon. The next morning I went to see the lady in question. It was a major's wife. She was not very ladylike. I had little Mikey with me and told her about our situation. I also assured her that I was able to do the work and that I could only work until we found a home of our own.

But she agreed. She told me that she had heard that the German maids were good workers and that they were known to be good cooks. Which was good, because she entertained a lot, since her husband was a doctor. I had a job and we had a place to stay. We moved in right away. There was a big nice and clean room with a bath upstairs for us just like they said, with a bed, table and two chairs. We lived out of suitcases for a while. This wasn't a problem, since we would not live there long.

When I came downstairs to start my job, it looked like she needed help badly. The house was a disaster. Actually, I didn't mind that at all. I could do no wrong here. I made up my mind right there to show her what I was made of. I was left alone most of the day to do what I thought was important. There were three children: two in grade school and a toddler at home.

In the morning Mikey and I went downstairs after CJ left. I saw the little fenced area where the small children played, situated just right. I could see the two little ones from just about every window and could do my work while they were safe. It was still a little hard not to be with them. Mikey watched the bigger children and everybody was nice to him. I was glad when somebody gave him a walker to move around in.

In no time at all, I had order in the house. The dishes washed from the night before, the floors cleaned, everything in its place. I had to hurry to find a little time with my son and friends.

The older children were taken care of and off to school. I felt that she was happy the way I worked but she never said it out loud.

Then things changed somewhat. My southern lady started sleeping in longer and longer and had a little bell by her bedside, which rang very often for me to wait on her.

I felt like a maid and did not like it since there were more important things for me to do. She started hiring me out to baby-sit for the neighbor children. She also would not allow me to wash my laundry in the machine anymore as she promised. We made up our minds not to stay there any longer.

One Sunday, which was my day off and my laundry day, I was washing all our things in the little bathroom sink by the window. It was a nice sunny day. I was thinking how unfair and ungrateful she was after I'd tried so hard. I could not help myself. I felt so sad I began to cry.

CJ came over and said, "Leave the rest of the laundry, let's go and see if we can afford a little car. Without one, we will be here forever."

We went by bus and came home with the biggest, oldest, most beautiful, Pontiac. The following week, we had found a little tiny house in Tillicum, very close to Fort Lewis. It was like a little summer cabin by the lake. A little old rowboat came with it. The cabin was very small and had cracks in it. You could see sunlight coming through at a certain time of the day. There was a garage right next to it about twice as large as our cabin and about ready to collapse. We could stay here as long as we wanted for very little rent. It was our home.

I dreaded what I had to do next. I knew I would have to go downstairs and quit my current job. I did go down but then lost my nerve. I should have given her time to find someone else. I remember doing the dishes from the night before thinking how I would explain it to her. She rang that little bell and later came into the kitchen. I dropped my sponge into the soapy water. The soap bubbles coming up like a fountain after it hit the water and I said, "I quit." I did not plan it like that, but it was said. I apologized for the way I said it and told her about the little house we found while driving around in our car.

She was angry and called her husband and I went upstairs and packed.

The following morning, I went downstairs. CJ did not go with me. I apologized again and told her I expected to be paid. She told me that she could not pay me until the following week. She gave me a going away present, which I did not expect, a cleaning bucket that leaked, plus a half empty box of body powder with a dirty puff. I left the "gifts" on her porch and a note that stated, "No thank you." We never went back. Maybe it was not the thing to do, but it made me feel better, it was hard to let the money go. We could have used it and I earned it but I did not have to say thank you again.

We celebrated by going to a restaurant for breakfast. Then we drove to our little natural air-conditioned villa by the lake. We first bought bedding, a used baby crib, a playpen, and a little swing for Mikey. We put the swing in the garden I started. It was a different life for the Burger family.

I remember the day when we discovered Mt. Rainier. We first thought it to be a cloud formation. It was the highest mountain I had ever seen. Soon after our discovery we packed a picnic basket full of goodies and drove as far as we could to see it. It was a beautiful mountain. We played in the snow, saw wild animals, and other unbelievable sights.

We were so happy. Each payday we bought a little something for the house; like pots, pans, dishes, towels, whatever was necessary. We even bought a big refrigerator which we had trouble getting into our tiny kitchen. The next thing we wanted was a much-needed washing machine. But that purchase had to wait since there was no room. Our home was the cutest little place once we got through with it. We lived there most of the summer. Finally we were informed that we had quarters at Fort Lewis.

At first I felt bad, leaving our first little home, but the quarters were a nice two-story apartment. Mikey had his own room, upstairs, right next to ours. There was a big living room and kitchen downstairs. We had electric heat and a stove, but no furniture. So we went downtown where we ended up at Sears. We bought everything necessary including a washing machine, the American way, a few dollars down and then so much a month. Life was good and we counted our blessings. Maybe you have to go through hard times to appreciate the good.

Living in Fort Lewis was very convenient for CJ and me. We shopped at the PX. We had nice neighbors and soon had many friends. I even met three more German war brides. They had similar stories to tell. We finally had to trade in our old, but not so faithful anymore, Pontiac. Papa said keeping it running was too expensive so we bought a brand new Pontiac.

The color I fell in love with was not on the lot so we ordered our new car. We thought it was absolutely beautiful and worth waiting for. I recall how happy and excited we were when the deal was made and we drove home. But this happiness was not to last. A few days later, everything changed again.

My husband was to go to Korea for a year. That was bad news. How was I to handle all the responsibility all alone, so soon? However, he was a soldier and should have expected most anything. I thought since he had been stationed in Germany so long, that we would be stateside together for a while.

It was a good thing that we were still able to cancel the new car. I could not drive and had no place to store it. I would also have to move out of the quarters.

Luck was with us. A neighbor told us of a place in Lakewood, where houses were being built, we went there right away. There were four of them just framed up.

We looked at the plans and walked through two ramblers and two Cape-Cod styles, which had two bedrooms down and an unfinished upstairs. We had to imagine it all, since the houses were just framed at the time. We picked one of the Cape-Cods, the one with the biggest backyard. This house was located on a little lane close to "Little Church on the Prairie." It was so simple in those days. If you had the closing cost of $400 and made $55 payments a month, you bought yourself a house. It was good to have a home instead of the new car.

Chapter 17
Fending for Ourselves While Papa is in Korea

Papa left us to go to Korea, so very far away. I realized now it was all up to me and that was scary. But now Mikey and I would soon have a home with a lot of planning to do.

We found out that we could stay in the Army quarters until the house was built. CJ was relieved and so was I. What would I do with the big car out there that was parked on the street? I never asked for any favors, so I learned to drive myself. I was not a good driver, but I was able to drive it from here to there, about five miles.

When the day came, Mikey and I prayed a lot and it seemed like that little guy knew that he had to be real good and quiet until we were actually "home."

All our furniture was left in the garage since our hardwood floors were still wet. We had to sleep in the kitchen two nights and then had a lot of fun.

I remember our radio was on and we were dancing after everything was in the house. We had a little party just for the two of us. I had a little problem bringing in the heavy stuff like the couch and most of all, that big refrigerator, because of the two steps from the garage into the kitchen, but I did it. We had nothing but time for everything from now on.

We missed Daddy a lot, but hard work made the time go faster.

After everything was settled inside, I went in the backyard with my spade and started to clean up between the property lines. Believe it or not, I spaded the whole area. It was a big job and took a long time. I was stubborn enough plus I knew what I was doing. I learned it when I was placed in Berlin when I was younger.

The result was great. The back yard looked bigger. I tied a rope around the whole area and it really looked good.

I knew when Pop came home he would be surprised and he was. I always dreamed about living in my own little house and planned on making it look special. When I woke up each morning it was a pretty good feeling.

A lady came to the house one day and asked me if I would take care of her little boy while she went to Texas for a few weeks. I didn't know her and was not sure why she came to me. I had never seen her before. We had coffee and talked for a while.

Mikey and Timmy, her little son, were instant friends. Hand in hand, Mikey showed him around the house. After awhile, I told her that I was happy to take care of that little fellow especially since the boys got along so good.

Before she left, she returned to my house with a bed, clothes, and toys and insisted on paying me for two weeks in advance and left.

Everything went so fast. I must admit that it was wonderful. Mikey had a little friend. Timmy liked us right away, and did not miss his mommy very much. I guess while his mommy was working, he was used to living with strangers.

Timmy's mom came back about a month later. She had married again and took Timmy with her. Christmas was coming and we had extra money to celebrate. We missed Timmy for a long time and wondered where he was. His mom promised to keep in touch with us but we never heard from them again.

Mikey and I kept missing Daddy and were waiting for him to come home. The house and the yard started to look pretty good except for the front. There had to be a pretty lawn before CJ came home plus a few other things like drapes and things. Our budget did not allow it. I found myself a job to earn some money.

I believe it was St. Joseph's Hospital where I applied first and was given a job as a nurse's aid from 11 p.m. to 7 a.m. Mikey could sleep with a little friend on our street. The arrangement was good with one exception. When I came home my little fellow was ready for the day and I needed to sleep. I worked there long enough to pay for the grass. That was enough and I decided not to work anymore.

A short time before my husband arrived home from Korea, I tried one more time to earn some money. I sort of had to. I had received two checks from the government and felt great. I decided right away to buy Mike a new bed. He was ready for a new one and I had seen one in the Sears catalog. I had waited for the day especially since his mattress was old and bad. This time he would get a brand new one.

The next morning Mikey and I went shopping. We spent a good part of the money on a brand new youth bed with a cowboy bedspread, a little table with chairs, and a record player he could manage on his own. The record player was a floor model with a few records like the Teddy Bears Picnic, one of his favorite songs. I recall the fun we had dancing around with excitement to celebrate in the pretty room. Our fun was short lived. We were shocked when the mailman came. We were told that a mistake had been made. There wouldn't be a check for the coming month or we would have to return the second check. I found myself a job the next morning and made arrangements for a live-in babysitter. I planned on working double time in a cannery.

My job was to line up washed and cut broccoli on a conveyor belt. The packer down the line could just grab a handful to put them in a box to be weighed. I did that for many hours. This was a very boring job. I fell asleep one night with my eyes open. I unconsciously placed a few dozen broccoli completely upside down. Oh yes, they all pointed the wrong way. When they arrived at the end of the conveyor, there was a loud outcry that woke up everybody on both sides of the line. What an experience working and sleeping at the same time.

Everybody started talking again for a while. Then there was silence, except for the noise from the machines. This started my dilemma in the first place.

I was not in trouble and nobody actually mentioned it anymore. Maybe it was not the first time somebody went daffy doing that, but I found myself another job.

By now, I was getting used to finding a new job. I heard of the PX looking for help and worked there behind the counter until my bills were paid.

It was a happy day when Mikey and I drove downtown to pick up Daddy at the train station. From now on everything just had to be okay. We had a nice home in a beautiful state and we were together again.

Since CJ was on leave for a while, he had time to do a lot of work at home. First he built a real nice fence all around the house. We then built a large cement patio to cover all the rocks I had dug up. Mikey now had a place large enough to ride his little tricycle. When we did not feel like working, we went either to the mountain or the ocean. Sometimes we just drove without a plan and always found new and interesting places.

I was pregnant again and happy about it. This time I hoped for a little girl.

When we started to talk about Mama in Luxembourg, it was CJ that said, "Do you think she would like to live with us?" I was so excited that he would say that. I wrote a letter right away that we are saving enough money for the plane or boat trip. Maybe that was a good idea, then again maybe not. I knew Mama was not the same anymore. Many people changed in those horrible war years. I thought she was tougher than that and would snap out of it once life was livable again.

But the fact that her son had died and the thought of how he had died must have been too much for her. She had brothers and sisters in Luxembourg but after awhile, she moved away and lived in one room by herself.

I was sure it would be good for her to come and live with us. It was not so easy to come up with the money right away. She just had to wait awhile since it was more then we could afford at that time.

I was three months pregnant when my husband had new orders. We had to move to Camp Roberts, California. I could have stayed at home but insisted on going. Now that I was with baby again I could not stay behind. The more we talked about it, the better we liked the idea.

Our furniture was stored and our house was for rent. We told Mama to wait. We would get her as soon as we were settled in California.

We also traded the old car for a new Kaiser-Fraizer. It was very hard to leave our lovely little home.

We wound through mountains, deserts, and places where palm trees and oranges grew. We ended up in San Miguel, which was close to Camp Roberts. This time it was worse then ever. We had no military quarters to live in. We moved into a real old and stinky trailer, since we could not afford to live in a hotel. Then we moved in with a little old man for a few days. He was nice but had a bad case of excess gas plus a few other bad habits. But what could we do? We were searching for a place every day and didn't think that our situation could get worse, but believe me, it did.

Mama was on her way to Camp Roberts, California. The telegram said that her papers were ready, and her brother had bought her a ticket for the ship Rheindam (out of Holland). What could we do now?

Mama knew hard times, that is for sure, and also learned that life had all kinds of downers. We had never sunk as low as that before.

Maybe we should have stayed at home, but as long as CJ was in the states, we should be together.

Everything would have been better in Tacoma. In California the weather was so hot, dusty, and dry. There were two of the most horrid creatures in the world, snakes and the biggest spiders. We also were blessed with cockroaches. We'd already had one earthquake right when arrived in 1952 and I was already as big as a house.

About this time, there was a big tragedy in Atascadero. A Mexican man had killed his wife in the desert. It seemed like everybody had heard of the tragedy. The children were taken away and placed in a home and their little shack, out in the desert, was empty.

We heard most of the details from a soldier's wife. She had inquired about the place and was able to rent it. When she heard that we were desperate, she offered to have us stay with them, until we could find something else.

She gave us the bigger of two rooms since my Mama was on the way. Mama was coming by boat and we knew it was impossible to find something else by then. There was one double bed where CJ and I, very pregnant, slept with Mikey in the middle. Along the other wall was a very narrow cot with a homemade mattress.

Mama came before we found another place. We had decided that when she came we would go back home but our house was already rented. We went to pick up Omi, my Mama, from the little train station. I don't know where it was, but it reminded me of old time movies.

And there she was. She looked fresh like a daisy while I felt so very bad, hot, and big. I don't remember what she said first. After hugging and gathering all her baggage, I tried to prepare her for the shock of her life. She told me not to worry. However, I could hear her thinking. I tried to convince her that this was just temporary.

I told her we had decided to ask the people now living in our house to please find another place since all of us are coming back home again.

Mama did not say much. It was all so different then we had planned. It was so hard on her and us. When she finally started talking, it was about Theo. Once she started she could not get off of the subject. To me, many times she sounded like she needed help. After awhile, I started to need help myself, as my husband didn't know what to think or do.

One day, CJ came home with good news. He'd found an apartment with one bedroom and large living room, in Atascadero. We moved right in and slept on the floor until our furniture came.

After our things came and we all had a bed again, things got better for all of us. It had been an incredible situation. The apartment was nice and clean and at last we all felt that we had a new lease on life.

In August 1952, a little earlier than expected, I was ready for the hospital that was about 40 miles from the apartment. We just had in mind to call a taxi, when CJ came home to check on me.

Oh, I was so scared about getting to the hospital in time, but now that he was home, everything would be all right.

We all went to the hospital at Camp Roberts and I had a beautiful little baby girl. We called her Doris Nanett.

Sure I yodeled a little like the doctor said I would, but she was worth it.

My Mama and Mikey were not allowed in the hospital and I was surprised seeing Mikey looking in the window. My Mama held him way up high so he could look in and see us. Now, we had fun again.

I was blessed with a healthy and happy baby and if I say so myself, good looking. Just like Mikey was. The way things were going we were still lucky in the most important things.

On the weekends we went to the beach with a large picnic basket and had good times. Mama had new friends. One was a German lady about her age and another lady who was a foot doctor. They liked each other and spent many afternoons together. Mama must have told one of them that she would like to find a part-time job to earn a little money on her own. Then she was introduced to another lady that owned or managed a small hotel where she was working in the sewing room. Later on she moved in with one of the ladies and we saw her only on the weekends.

We had good times then. Everybody was happy. CJ and I had a long conversation one day, about the way we lived and what we went through. We wondered what we would do if he suddenly would be transferred again. That's when he told me that he was thinking about leaving the Army.

We were going back home to Tacoma, Washington. We still had no news about our house, or any idea how soon we would be able to move. Then we received a letter from our real estate agent. Our renters were in the process of moving. Over and over I had to tell Mikey about the green grass and shady trees. I told him about his room, the pretty backyard, and the little garden that we were going to make. I also told him about the room his little sister would have.

I was a little worried about Daddy finding a job but he kept saying, "If a fellow really wants to work he will find a job, don't worry."

We were happy to go home, all of us. Especially after we learned we lived very close to an institution for the criminally insane, in Atascadero.

CJ made up his mind not to reenlist after he asked me again what I thought. As much as we all longed to go home, we no longer had to think about it.

Mama stayed a few weeks longer. She liked her job and her friends especially since we were not sure how long it would take, until we could actually move in again.

Some good friends of ours, Hedy and Lee, at Fort Lewis, invited us to stay with them until we could move into our home. Hedy and Lee made us feel welcome. Some of our other friends were stationed in Germany and there they lived in nice homes and had houseboys and maids. They paid them 25 cents an hour.

Mama arrived in Tacoma. She had her own room now and we showed her the most beautiful state in the USA.

Chapter 18
Never a Dull Moment

It was not as easy to find a job as CJ thought. He started going to night school to be a builder and by day did odd jobs. Whatever came up, he still found time to finish the upstairs and whatever needed to be done. I believed there was nothing he could not do.

My husband was a builder and he proved it. It did not take long until he started his own business building cabinets.

I'll never forget the day he told me our garage would be his workshop for a while. His cabinets were beautiful and much better then the ones in our house. I knew that someday he would build us new ones his way.

Business got better. There were many new houses being built all around and since his work was very good, he had plenty to do.

Then CJ bought an older house about four blocks from home. It was zoned for business on a big lot. He tore out the inside and started working there. I counted my blessings and thanked God. There was no more sawdust coming into the house from the garage and our new car had a home at last. At first, he remodeled and worked on new editions but more and more he concentrated on cabinets.

"Home and Store Cabinets and Fixtures" was written on his new van. He felt good doing what he did. His customers were happy and the word was out from previous good work and advertising in the newspaper.

Mikey started kindergarten right next to the little grade school very close to our home. It seemed everybody, even the little girls, liked Mikey. He was a good student.

His first little girlfriend came home with him for lunch one day. I remember watching them, when they were just about at the house. She was bashful and Mikey assured her that she did not have to be afraid. Mikey introduced her to me and I must say that she was a pretty little thing. I think it was from that day on when he called me Mom instead of Mommy.

He came home from school one day and told me that she had to move to Walla Walla, Washington to live with her grandma. He talked about her for some time after that. Once he told me he liked her so much because she was so pretty and her blond hair would flow when she skipped.

With the next little girlfriend he was engaged. He told me after I found my only diamond ring in his blue jeans pocket. I was so surprised when I saw it among nails, candy wrappers, and rubber bands.

I talked to him about it. He told me with a sigh, he had been engaged to her, but asked to get the ring back since they broke up. I had not missed the ring since I did not wear it when I worked in the garden.

He actually didn't feel like he had done anything wrong until I told him and then he was sorry. I still think about that little girl with my engagement ring hanging on her necklace. I don't know how long she had it or why her mom never saw it.

Nothing like that happened again and about twenty years later, when our house was robbed, I lost the ring anyway. The ring was not very expensive but had many memories.

Little Doris was a doll. When she was about three years old she disappeared. We could not find her anywhere. I could not understand how she could get out of the backyard. It was not like her to go anywhere without telling me. I held up pretty good at first but called the Sheriff right away.

He checked everything in and around the house and then told me to stay home, by the phone. Soon it started to get dark outside and I really started to worry. I saw people searching for her in the fields across the street. Now and then the phone rang but so far, no good news. I was surprised how many people were alert and trying to find her in such a short time. Many people called to find out what she looked like and what kind of clothes she was wearing.

Then the Sheriff came back and searched the house again. He asked me if we had any footlockers and I froze. We had two. They were filled up and way under the rafters. He checked them and before he came down, he opened the closet door once more. There she was, sleeping in the corner with her little blankie. It was very hot in the closet. The first thing she said was, "I was hiding so Mikey can't find me and then my eyes went twinkle and now I would like to have a cup of tea." Why tea, I'll never know. Everybody laughed and I fell apart. I often wondered why I did that. There were so many things going on those days with our little girl. There is one more story I remember so well when she was about the same age.

She came home from Sunday school very angry and excited. I knew right away that she was angry, because of the way she always expressed herself. With both hands and arms toward the back, she informed me that she did not like God anymore. Her Sunday school teacher said that God told one Daddy to take a knife and kill his little boy and then burn him all up. We had to straighten her out about that in a hurry. We knew what the story was all about. But this person had no business teaching it. It was good to know that she was listening and came home to tell us about it so we could explain it.

Sometime not too much later, she told me that she heard a very dirty joke. Oh boy! I had to hear about that.

Well it was like a riddle when she asked me, "What did one burp say to the other burp?" Now I was a little relieved and asked her, "So what did one burp say to the other burp." With her arms toward her back she told me, "Let's be stinkers and go out the back door." She always did that when she explained something important.

I kept a memory box in the attic with all kinds of stories since there was so much going on then. I did not want to forget. We never had a dull moment, but also never a problem we could not handle.

Mama decided to rent a little house. She wanted Mimi, her husband, and Ted (then fifteen years old) to come and live with her. Lotti did not want to come. She was now over eighteen and engaged to be married.

We were plenty worried about that idea but it came together. I noticed for sometime that Mama wanted to have the last word on any decisions the way she was used to. Tension was growing between CJ and Mama.

Mama had her wish and was she happy.

We found work for Mimi and her husband. Ted was enrolled in school and all of us were relieved. We lived close to each other and were happy.

Erni and Mimi

I had joined the garden club where I met a nice bunch of ladies. We were called the Garden Neighbors and we were very active in many things. We went to lectures, and once a year traveled to conventions. The rest of our time, we worked for garden shows where we created the most beautiful flower arrangements for shows and special occasions. We had bazaars at Christmas to make money for different charities, etc. I was pretty good at floral arrangements. I was even elected president one year. I still have a drawer of blue ribbons.

Mike was about nine years old when I decided to become den mother for the Cub Scouts and enjoyed the best bunch of boys. We met once a week in our house. Doris was selected by everyone to be our mascot. We planned our doings without a problem.

There is not much we didn't do. We went to different factories to see how things were made, visited a few bakeries where every boy had cookies, went on hikes, and to ballparks. When it rained we had a workshop or just had fun with games.

They even built their own clubhouse with a flag that flew from the top. We had a big glass window and door in the front plus enough room for all of us to sit around the table inside.

When Mike was 11 years old, a little young yet, but determined, he was given a paper route.

I was a little worried at first. It was winter, still dark outside in the morning, and in the rainy season for which Washington State is famous. He had spunk and a good bike.

Only once I heard him complain when a big truck drenched his papers as it drove by. The papers were soaked and he got in trouble by an elderly man who always liked him before. I remember that and don't complain if the paperboy is late or misses us once in awhile. His second payday he handed me six dollars to buy myself a dress and said, "For six dollars including the tax." He was very proud whenever I wore it and so was I. We were truly blessed with two loving children in a time when the parents were still in charge.

Chapter 19
My Secret Dream to Visit my Family

I had just about given up my secret dream to see the old country again when CJ decided that we could afford the trip.

He had just finished a big job and told me to plan on it. He actually gave me the green light to get ready and tell everyone in Germany that I was coming for a visit. I was to fly from Seattle to Frankfurt.

CJ came home one day with bad news. He could not collect for the job for a long time because of a long sad story. I'd felt like this many times before. I had my passport and my suitcase packed and my balloon was burst again, and this time in a big way.

I got to go anyway. We borrowed the money from the bank on a "fly now and pay later" plan and had a wonderful time.

Charlott and Heinz were waiting for me and it was so good to see them and my old country again.

I am sure that I will never forget March 28, 1966. The sun was shinning and even though we drove on the Autobahn, I knew exactly where we were.

They now lived in Freiburg (Black Forest) and had a fantastic apartment on the sixteenth floor with an unbelievable view.

Heinz was proud to show me all the buildings that he was involved with. He was now a respected architect. Now and then on our trips to places we used to live, like Bruchsal, we noticed new buildings where friends of ours lived and died. But those moments were reminders and hurt never the less.

Everybody seemed very happy, busy, and content.

Lotti and I

With storks on the steeple

We drove all over Germany, Switzerland, and France in a little Volkswagen Bug. Wherever there was singing, yodeling, and good food, we joined in. We ate schnitzel and drank beer and I ordered white asparagus, which I love, and ate it until I did not want anymore.

Wherever we went to visit, it was obvious you had to drink wine, especially since everybody made their own. I was never tipsy. Maybe it looked like I was. My cheeks were glowing all the time. We were in wine country and you just had to have a glass because everybody insisted that theirs was the best.

It is hard to love two countries that you call yours because you have to say goodbye to one or the other.

On the flight back to the United States, I recall sitting in my assigned seat smiling a lot to myself and wondering what people were thinking whenever they looked at me. I didn't care, I felt good and the world might as well have known it.

Right there, I decided that my children were going to see the old, but pretty, country and meet its people. It was important to me.

115

I had been there for three weeks and had so many stories to tell. I was proud again and they had to know about it.

Soon we would be in Seattle. The weather was beautiful. I was buckled up and looking out of the window. And here it was "Seattle" in its glory. It was such a beautiful sight that I felt like crying. I do not cry a lot, and I think you probably know what I mean. I felt like telling somebody to put it to music. Something like "Coming back home to Seattle" seeing it like that. But first it had to be experienced. If only the young folks would sing more about the beautiful things they are proud of instead of all the trash that's allowed nowadays.

"Oh boy!" My husband would say, "Here she goes again." Well, don't you agree with me?

There they were, waiting for me. I felt so lucky when we arrived home. I found everything in tip-top shape. Everything was in order and I felt a little disappointed because it looked like I was not missed at all. Later I found out that it was not always so polished and nice. When I was due home, all of them pitched in and did a super job.

Mama seemed to be happy now and my vacation was not over yet. We drove together through the Olympic Mountains. I admit they were even better than what I saw in Germany. I agreed, it was different and there was more of it. We had good times and absolutely no more big problems.

When we worked we worked hard and when we had a chance to travel, we were just as tired in the evening.

Chapter 20
Building a Cabin

Pop had read in the Tacoma newspaper that there was land to be sold all around Summit Lake, very close to Rock Candy Mountain. We knew it well. We'd had good times there hunting for mushrooms, mostly Chanterelles (Pfifferlings) which I knew of since the day I could walk.

So we went to see if we could have a piece of that wonderland.

The lake was absolutely breathtaking. Three miles long, clear, clean, and spring fed. It was so quiet, all you could hear were the waves hitting the shore, some birds and a few bees buzzing around. It was so peaceful and beautiful that we all fell in love with it.

A nice wide road went all around the lake. I don't think I saw any houses or cabins yet except at the very end of the lake. The realtor showed us around. There was land for sale on both sides of the street and we found a place right by the water with an unbelievable view.

We could see the entire lake and it was very reasonably priced. They asked fourteen hundred and nineteen dollars for it; twenty dollars down and twenty dollars a month. We had 60 feet of waterfront and 300 feet up the hill to the road. "Yes," our minds were made up. We never regretted it. It was a jungle by the water, all overgrown with trees and bushes. We decided to start cleaning the beach first, just as soon as possible.

From then on we went up there every weekend to work. The whole family was involved.

There was a large flat area half way up the hill where we pitched our brand new tent and placed our big picnic table. It was large enough for all of us. Later on we built our new outhouse there.

The hole for the outhouse had to be dug very deep. Our children did most of that job. I truly believe that we had the best outhouse by the lake. We painted it snow white inside with washable paint. There was an electric light, sink with running water, and cabinets on the wall with our toothbrushes etc. We also had a place for cleaners and deodorant and no one was to throw anything but paper in that pit.

Everybody knew the rules before they went in there and everything was fine until John, Doris's friend carelessly dropped a pop can down in the hole.

Pop saw it while he was sanitizing and talked with that young man. Everybody thought it was funny and poor little John was a little embarrassed.

They were joking around and made a poem to hang on the wall as a warning. It went like this:

> "John, John what have you done
> you threw a pop can in the John
> it must now lay in the deep pit
> and soon be covered with all
> kinds of stuff."

Well, it was funny enough to leave it hanging for some time and even John smiled when he remembered.

Every weekend we worked until everything was prepared so we could start on our cabin. Mike already knew a lot about building since he had helped Pop a lot in the shop to earn money for a little motor scooter he needed to deliver newspapers and later a car. It was to be a simple cabin and turned out very nice with a big porch overlooking the water with two little rooms downstairs, a dressing room, and a place for a lawnmower and fishing stuff.

After our long dock was built with my fishing bench on the very end, right over the best known fishing hole, we were actually going up there just to have fun and rest.

Soon cabins were built everywhere. You could hear the builders working, and smell and see the brush being burned.

I imagined once, how it must have been when the first immigrants arrived in this country. Surely, there was someone living here at that time. It was too beautiful not to be found. We met new neighbors and life was good.

The work was done and our children were now teenagers. We all worked hard and a reward was due. But could we afford it?

Pop bought a speedboat and water skies for both kids. Doris and I were waiting on the cabin porch with binoculars in hand. We had waited a long time looking to the end of the lake where most boats were launched. We could never get a boat down our hill. There was no way to build a road and everything we used to build had to be carried down the long row of steps.

I remember Doris yelling, "Here they are!" She handed me the binoculars and I saw Pop and Mike putting our brand new boat in the water.

They were far away, but I could see what they were doing. The boat was light blue and white with a lot of chrome, which glistened in the sun. It was beautiful. It seemed it took forever to arrive and it was a lot of fun just looking at their faces. Such excitement!

Later that day we watched them from the porch taking turns water skiing.

That evening Pop and I had a long slow ride all around the lake to investigate where all our neighbors lived.

We found a tiny shack on an old dock that was used for a little store. I remember they had fishing worms in the refrigerator right next to the food. We never bought anything from there, only ice cream.

I drove there by myself many times but never bought worms since we fished with canned corn. Fish tasted better that way. At least I think so. We caught a lot of fish with just corn.

On Thanksgiving we came with our already stuffed turkey ready for the oven. We had a nice fireplace, stove, refrigerator, four bunks, a couch, a sink, water, and heater. There was a corner bench with a table like the ones they have in the old country, all in one room, but nicely arranged. We would go stomping around in the snow for hours, and come back hungry when the turkey was ready and smelled so good.

My friend Mary and her husband came up many times to fish and hunt mushrooms with us.

Before Christmas we came and baked our Christmas cookies.

One time after Mary and I were through baking, we decided to go for a little walk and while we were gone, our husbands, CJ and Dick, ate about half of our Christmas treasure. I can still see them both sitting by the fireplace and our Hutzelbrot in front of them, smiling as we came in. Like a couple of little boys being caught.

We've lost Dick since but Mary and I remember those days and talk about them often.

Mike finished high school and after graduation he decided to join the US Navy. A Navy recruiter, at the mall told him, that he would receive a good education plus the chance to see the world. He would also have time to decide what to do for the rest of his life.

He looked so good in this Navy blues when he came home, before he was shipped to the Philippines. Our son had changed some. I thought he was even better looking, maybe a little more reserved, but still very loving.

His time at home went by so fast and soon he had to leave again. Mama decided to come with us to the airport early the next morning. I told her that I would pick her up very early since we had to drive all the way to Seattle. She had told me to knock hard on the door in case she could not hear me, and to knock on the bedroom window also.

I did that, but she did not answer the door. Then I woke up her landlady next door and we both decided to break into the house to see what was wrong.

Mama was still in bed but unconscious. We called the ambulance and were told that she'd had a stroke during the night. She never saw or talked to us again. Pop and I went to the hospital while the rest of the family went to the Seattle Airport with Mike. It must have been hard on the boy to leave at a time like that. He loved his Omi very much. Ten days later my Mama died.

Now we had to plan the funeral and that was so very hard to do. I loved her so much. I hope I never have to go through something like that again. Our son came back for

121

the funeral. How exactly that was possible, I don't know, but I prayed for the one that made it possible. It made me feel like our son was in good hands since the Navy cared that much to send him home for the funeral of his Omi.

After the funeral, Mike went back to the Philippines but he wrote home often. We exchanged cassette tapes to tell each other what was going on here and there.

That is how we found out that he had a friend over there. A girl he'd met and we'd had many serious talks about. Our boy loved that girl and married her there.

We never thought his young bride would arrive in the U.S. before he was able to come home. But, one night while on guard duty he mentioned being all alone in the building. It must have been on a weekend when everybody else was in town. He told me then that they were expecting a baby and he wanted to have her in the states as soon as possible. So he sent her home to us.

When the day came, we were there at the airport to welcome Lety, our daughter-in-law, home. We had a snapshot of her and identified her right away. At home we showed her the two rooms that were all ready for the three of them. The baby furniture and other baby things she liked a lot. In fact, she told us that she was very happy to live with us. We got along just fine. After Mike came home, the fellows started to build a third room upstairs which turned out very nice. Mike worked with his dad and then our first grandchild was born.

We all went to the hospital and came home with a beautiful baby boy I called Benjie. That was the first name they had picked and I kept on calling him that even to this day (with permission).

He was sweet, beautiful, and bright as a penny. A few months later they bought the house next door. That reminded me of something my son once told me when he was still very small. We were talking about him getting married someday. I told him it could be possible that his wife to be would be already living somewhere.

He always listened and thought about what I said. He wanted to know if he could stay with us forever. I told him that he would have his own house by then. He thought about it again and said, "I know! Then we'll move next door."

Believe it or not, he moved into the house he pointed to and still lives there now. Whenever I think about that day, I know the exact place where he said it, and what he looked like at the time. They had two more boys, David and Danny. Also lovely and bright and good looking little characters.

In the meantime, Doris had done her thing. Even before she graduated from high school, she was running a little doughnut shop in the afternoon, mostly by herself. Later she clerked in different department stores and then worked as a bank teller. She saved her money and bought herself a little blue convertible MG.

She looked good in it and kept it shining all the time. It sure came in handy after the bank moved her around to different branches and also out of town.

She left us for a time but moved back home after Mike moved next door. There she met a friend of Mike's, named Chuck, who we all loved right away.

They were married and also had boys, Robby and Mikey, two little firecrackers with energy that never stopped. Don't you think we had good reason to be proud?

Rob and David

Benjie, David, Mike, and Rob

The Fun Bunch

We had a lot of fun together at the lake especially since all the work was done and now we just went for fun. The grandchildren were good swimmers. They'd been taught at the YMCA since they were babies.

One day after that long drive, we found out that we had been broken into. There are evil people in this world everywhere. Some of them found our little cabin and vandalized it. The cabin door was wide open and broken. Whoever did this not only came to steal, but completely vandalized our little place of happiness. There was broken dishes and garbage everywhere.

Pop's fishing boat was hit with a hatchet, the food was partially eaten, and the rest like coffee grounds, honey, and tuna fish was poured over our bathing suits. There were also a lot of things from cabins nearby. The place was full of our neighbor's belongings. One of our neighbors did not have a stove or fireplace. They found a hole right in the middle of the floor where they had a fire. It was real bad. They could have burned down the whole place.

They must have ended up in our place and stayed there at least one night according to the police. It was very sad for all of us.

After the neighbors were informed by phone, they came and collected what was theirs and all we did that day was clean up and hunt for things, which were either stolen or broken.

The following weekend somebody had broken all the windows and ruined the lawn by riding around in circles with motorbikes and they left a lot of garbage.

I did not like to stay there anymore and told it to one of our neighbors. They most likely had spread the word because just a few days later, we had phone calls asking if we would sell.

We talked about it and did. Since nobody could come and guard it, we sold it. At that time I did not care. But after the deal was made, we missed the place very much.

The new owners, a very nice elderly Italian couple, told us that we could come and go fishing anytime. We saw it again, one time, just driving by. For a long time we all missed our little cabin by the lake.

Chapter 21
Belated Honeymoon in Germany

My husband was always a hard worker. When he was not on his regular job, he worked on something at home, which I appreciated a lot. We both needed to get away from it all and decided to spend some time in Germany. I called it a very late honeymoon, to rekindle the past.

It was so nice. We drove to Bruchsal and saw the house I once lived in. We looked at the garden gate where we kissed good night after our dates. We sat on the bench where we first met and just visited old familiar places.

Heinz was so nice, he drove us anywhere we liked and even offered to take us on a trip to Venice, Italy for unforgettable memories. We decided to fly back again three years later.

On our second trip we had quite a delightful experience. We drove from one country to the next and did not have to show a pass. Nobody asked for identification. That was such a good feeling. All gates were open again.

Everything was built up again in the West. Many houses that I had seen totally destroyed were there again, identical but new. I felt as if I had awakened from a bad dream. People were friendly and hospitable. We visited everybody and were invited back by all. Nobody talked about the war anymore or the bombs. It was a happy country again with good people. I was proud.

It was springtime; we saw the storks resting on the rooftops. They had just made their yearly trip all the way from Africa. It is said that when storks nest on your roof, it brings good luck. Often, a new wagon wheel is placed on different houses in an attempt to attract the storks. However, the birds seem to find the same roof year after year.

My niece Christa called us from Zurich. She invited us to meet her and her husband Freddy in Sem.

We were all excited to go there. Charlott had already told us about this place way up in the Pyrenees, a beautiful mountain home between France and Spain.

When we arrived there we felt like we were lost in time. "Sem" is a very small village, a little summer retreat, nestled in the high mountains with an incredible view. Surely, it is one of the oldest and most hidden away places that I have ever seen with very narrow streets, just wide enough for a cart. They actually had a Burgermiester there. We met him and were invited to drink a glass of wine with him. He was a pleasant older man who had a lot of stories to tell.

I could have listened to him for hours but we had some investigating to do. We found an old cemetery, which was well kept and noticed many beautiful flowers, which were made out of old beads. There we met an English lady that invited us later for tea. She also was very nice and interesting to be with. There was only one more person there, a young man. He was there to look after those places while the owners were absent. He lived all alone up there and spoke English and was very pleasant. He also invited us for coffee and some kind of pastry. I watched him take it from a cupboard and then trying to scrape something off it by the sink. There was no way to get rid of all the ants on it. We felt so bad about that, since he really tried so hard to do something nice for us.

Then we found the large ceremonial rock that we read about, a celtic sacrificial alter. Charlott, Christa, and I did not stay long. It gave us goose bumps, but the boys stayed and had a good time there. Somehow, that did not seem right.

It was a wonderful vacation but, then came the time to fly back home to Washington. After landing in Seattle, we noticed a group of children dressed up as clowns with balloons and a large sign that said, "Welcome Omi and Grandpa." They'd come for us! All of them wanted to come with Doris to pick us up.

We arrived late and the boys were tired from waiting so long but recovered fast. A lot of work went into this, but no doubt, it paid off. It was surely a nice way to be greeted home. They did real good.

Chapter 22
The Costume Shop

In 1978 Doris and I had an idea to start a little gift shop right in front of Pop's business. It was a big area. After long talks, my husband agreed to look into the possibilities.

Soon after, we had permission. He started to build and it ended up the cutest little gift shop. We named it The Sandpiper. Pop did it all in a short time with the help of our son Mike. It was really nice inside and out. We even had a little old fashioned sweet shop and a good variety of handmade articles to offer. We visited and shopped in the wholesale houses until we truly believed that we were special.

At Christmastime it was the loveliest place to find those special gifts and shop around. We served coffee and cookies and were a little disappointed because we expected more customers.

We were hidden away and hard to find without advertising which we could not afford. But we did not give up. We kept on working and dreaming.

On the following Halloween, we decided to decorate. We found some real good masks plus a few other creepy things. At that time business was bad and since there was not much to do, I started to sew a few costumes for sale. One lady saw what I was doing and ordered an Indian squaw outfit. I think she loved that little papoose and the beadwork. It did turn out especially nice. She had asked me at first if she could rent it and "Bingo!" Once I started, there was no end to them. Somehow the word was out, and we were in the costume business. The costumes got better and better. It was unbelievable. I could not make costumes fast enough. We had orders for theaters, schools, and different organizations. I even got to make the first Tacoma Dome Turtle. We needed more room and had to use the garage next to Pop's shop to store the orders. The shelves there were filled while we got going and slowly removed the gifts. We took out the cute sweet shop. Nobody bought goodies and so we had to eat it all up ourselves.

We were actually needed and had something that the public liked.

Once a year we had a costume party in the backyard of our house. All the family, employees, and friends came to model the new costumes for the following year. They all were photographed and placed in a large book where the customers had a chance to select the perfect costume. Those parties were always a hit and my husband usually known as quiet and reserved, turned out to be the biggest ham.

After awhile, Pop decided to quit building cabinets and joined us. We had all the room we needed. He combined the two buildings and then we had room enough to hang close to 3,000 costumes the following year. Plus accessories. We also put some money into the business until we had everything we needed and hired help. I could go on and on telling about how exciting it was to know that we were found and that we are actually needed on Halloween,

Christmas, Fashing, Easter, St. Patrick's Day, and of course there were the theatres and the clowns.

We gave clown lessons and visits to birthday parties in the craziest costumes. Our daughter can handle anything and loves it. And my husband of all people studied make-up. I heard him through the speaker once explaining how to use make-up. I never knew he had it in him. It was high time for him to join the fun. Actually, from then on we lived for that, now much bigger, fun box in Lakewood now called Lakewood Costumes.

Grandpa and Omi

Party Goers

Grandpa in costume

Grandpa as a Cheerleader

David, Mike, Rob, and Grandpa

138

In 1983 I met a real nice person name Bessie. She was interested in helping me in the sewing department. After Lety and our son divorced and both were remarried, I had worked there alone for a while and needed help badly. Now I had a good and willing hand plus an instant friend. Bessie must like to work for us because she is still with us at Lakewood Costumes.

Thanks to her and the Lakewood Library, where I studied period costumes, because I was not a learned seamstress, we had all kinds of costumes. From cavemen, through most of the centuries, and later space beings, character animals, and whatever was called for. We worked hard together but also had fun doing what we did. Once I had an idea and the material for it, I would cut out the garment, pin it together, and Bessie finished it.

Oh we had plenty of problems in the beginning, before the stores had patterns. Especially the Shakespearean gowns (remember?), but in time we did real good together, "Didn't we Bessie?"

A few years later we had a little granddaughter Joline from Mike's second marriage. She was a very pretty little girl who turned into a lovely young lady.

Joline in the house her Daddy built

Joline and friend

Chapter 23
A Trailer Trip with the Grandsons

All of us still missed our regular trip to the cabin by the lake, especially the grandchildren. After we traded our small trailer for a much larger one including two sets of bunk beds, we planned to take a trip with all five grandsons. There was excitement again. There was room for all of us to sleep. I remember when we all decided how it would be best. Benjie and Robby were in the upper bunks, Omi and Grandpa were in the lower bunks, Danny was on a mattress in a sleeping bag between us on the floor, and Mikey and David had plenty of room on the long cushions from the dining area after collapsing the table. So far so good. After all their clothes and whatever else was tucked away, we were on our way.

First stop, Sunshine Point at Mount Rainer, right next to the river. Our adventure had now begun but it started to rain. As soon as we were parked, the door opened and everybody was out and down to the river in the rain. Soon they were all wet and muddy. Well, by the time they had changed their clothes, the clean clothes were mixed in with the muddy ones. I knew we had to have an understanding of what clothes went where. I do not remember too much more about the rest of the evening, but I do recall the next morning when the Burger boys were wearing long flannel nightshirts, and the Hayden boys had on their pj's. All of them were standing in a circle around the water faucet brushing their teeth. What a precious sight. I should have taken a picture.

The rain stopped the next day. We drove up the mountain and played in the snow for a while. We continued, and sang heading toward the Columbia River. The weather was wonderful. We stopped at a very nice trailer park. There was a little lake where we rented paddleboats. But first we had to have a talk around the large picnic table. We decided laundry needed doing first since everything was a big mess. So, we stuffed all the dirty clothes into a big sack and we went to the Laundromat. I must have sounded like an Army sergeant, telling the boys how it had to be done. But they all decided to cooperate and they actually had fun. The boys did such a good job we decided to rent two of the paddleboats for a couple of days.

Next to our campsite was a tent. It was closed up and quiet while we had been sorting and packing clothes. Somebody in the tent started to laugh out loud. What we did not know was that all the while we had been sorting and packing clothes, they had been listening. They looked out and asked me if I was the boys' grandma. They said, "We think you deserve a medal." I was a little embarrassed, at first, since this was a private affair.

Then we were on the road again. Everybody had a lot of fun. Benjie kept all of us entertained while we were driving with new songs and riddles and then we ended up with 99 Bottles of Beer on the Wall. I was glad to tell them that the Columbia River was in sight (no more Beer on the Wall after that). We found a beautiful trailer park in Vantage, right by the river and not only that, there was an indoor pool close by. There they had a chance to show off all their swimming and diving tricks. Grandpa and I were very impressed and proud of every one of them, even Danny, the little one. We came home with good and lasting memories.

Chapter 24
Doris and I Visit Europe

It was Doris' turn to visit Europe and it was the right time, in the middle of June while the costume shop was in its slow season. My sister Mimi decided to come with us as she needed to see her daughter and grandchildren again. Those were exciting days for all of us.

We flew to Zurich, Switzerland. First to meet them all and then we drove in two cars through the countryside home to Freiburg. It was so good to see everybody again. We said goodbye for a short time so Mimi could spend some time with her daughter.

From then on Heinz was our driver again and we were constantly on the road for new adventures.

While in Baden-Baden with Lotti, we visited her in-laws. That was nice. They lived very close to where we used to live and grew up. Their house was about ten minutes away from there and very interesting. They lived in an old but stately house with a little hide-away room built way on top. Up there one could step out through a small door to a ledge and walk all around a little room. From there we could see our old neighborhood. We were standing there when suddenly the big bells from our church close by started to ring. It was a loud, powerful sound that startled us all. We stood quietly, until they were silent again.

The next day we went to our old church. It was so beautiful there. Although it was empty and quiet, it was still full of memories. I felt like a little child again.

All of us sat in a pew right next to the confessional. It was right there where I confessed my sins as a child many times.

So many memories went through my mind. Heinz was sitting right next to me and while we whispered to each other, I remembered something else. Something I'd never told anyone before. In a low voice I told him that it was in the very same confessional, on a Saturday, I was to go in there to tell our chaplain about my wrongdoings. I absolutely did not know what to tell him since I could not think of anything bad that I had done that week. But I was sure that he would not believe me so I picked a sin at random from my little book. It was about forbidden sex. I went right in there and confessed that I was guilty of looking, talking, and doing that. (Mama had never explained that one to me or anybody else that I remembered). It was called keusch heit (chastity).

Heinz started to laugh out loud which was not to be done in a big empty church like that. Later, when we talked about it at home, Charlott remembered another story that had to do with this church.

Every Sunday at eleven a.m., Mama, Mimi, Theo, Charlott, and I walked to church and often we were late even though it was only a fifteen-minute walk there. Mama had a thing about handkerchiefs, clean teeth, and messed up hair. So we walked back home to straighten up. On this particular Sunday, we were late again. Our priest was up on the pulpit already preaching, when we walked in right through the middle of the aisle to our usual place way in the front. He stopped talking and in a low voice said, "ja, when you are here, then all of us are present." Not very loud but we heard it and so did the whole congregation I am sure. Yes, our Mama was a little eccentric. But not to be ashamed of, only a little embarrassed.

Before we left Baden-Baden, I wanted to see my old school house. It used to be a beautiful majestic stone building. I had a lot of bad, but also a few good memories from there. But it was no more. Instead, I found a very modern, ugly building made mostly of glass. Then we walked to the house we used to live in on a pretty boulevard with two rows of trees and benches. All that was also gone. Now our house is right next to a very busy street with an overpass. All in the name of progress I guess.

It was good that Mimi came with us that year. Soon after, her doctor informed us that she had Alzheimer's. We all wondered why she had changed so much. Now I am so very sorry that I sometimes accused her of getting mean. I feel plenty bad about that. Mimi passed away on September 6, 1989, in an awful nursing home, a place I will never forget.

Chapter 25
Lakewood Parade – Second Blue Ribbon

Pop and Mike

It was good to be back home again. The costume shop was getting ready for the yearly Summerfest Parade in Lakewood. A lot of work was ahead of us. Everybody from the shop and a number of good friends were involved in this event and we all loved it. It was the second year for us and I was in charge of decorating the flatbed and organizing all the costumes everyone was to wear, from those in the wagon to those who walked.

We decorated the flatbed "float" with balloons and many of our friends dressed in our best costumes. We had received the blue ribbon the year before and were trying for it a second time. We got it!

Omi with the Blue Ribbon

Chapter 26
Mike's Turn to Visit Europe

I'd been counting my blessings for a long time. We are all well and have good family ties which is very important to me. I do not move so fast anymore since arthritis got a hold of me.

My head keeps telling me about all the things I still would like to accomplish, but my body does not want to cooperate.

In 1994 I decided it was high time to make that trip to Germany with my son (the workaholic). He never had the time to go back to where he was born. But he made it happen this time. We flew together to Frankfurt and decided to take the train to Freiburg, which was very nice for me.

Heinz was there at the station to take us home. His little trailer was already packed for traveling. Mike and I slept in the trailer, while Heinz stayed in his "Hotel-Opel" (his car) at night in a very comfortable bed.

Everything was so organized. We ate real good since he was quite a connoisseur and did all the cooking while we were on the road.

Charlott did not come with us this time but Heinz called her once a day to inform her where we were and that we were okay. That brother-in-law is an okay guy in my book, but I knew that when they'd first met.

Our three weeks went much too fast. It was a nice visit and we had a good time wherever we went.

While we were on our way home, flying over the big puddle (the Atlantic Ocean), Mike was so impressed with my beautiful country and its people that I felt like the fat cat that just ate a fat mouse.

Chapter 27
Golden Anniversary and Retirement

On December 10, 1998, CJ and I had our golden anniversary. To think that fifty years ago both of us went to the Burgermeister in Bruchsal to get married. It was not exactly the wedding a girl dreams of, but in those days we had daily disappointments. That was fifty long years ago.

We knew that our children had something special planned for us. I kind of expected that the whole family and everybody from Lakewood Costumes would be there to celebrate since they had a hall rented at the Lakewood Elks. I was right, a hall was needed but when we got there it seemed very quiet. I wondered where the people were located. I remember climbing up those outside stairs. Since my arthritis was bad that day it took me a little while to get up the steps and it seemed like the door was hard to open, but when it did, there was an ocean of people.

I believe, close to everybody I knew was there. My old neighbors, whom I had not seen in years, came from

Spokane with their three daughters. Also friends from Tacoma who I had not seen in a long time were there. The more the place lit up, the more long lost friends appeared. Then I spotted CJ's brothers and wives. Ed and Mary from Nevada; Ivan and Ruth from California; and Raymond and Pat from Chicago. It was mind-boggling. Later, when I saw myself and Pop on the video, I thought I looked mentally disturbed with my mouth wide open.

When the hugging and kissing was temporarily over, we noticed the long table of food. Of course that was Bessie's doing. She's been my dear friend for years and was my helper in creating the costumes for the Merry Makers. The food was absolutely delicious. There was so much of it. Everybody was hungry since it took so long to get started. Later there was music and dancing. There was also a slide show of Pop and I on a large screen. Danny and his friends performed their break dancing for us. It was just incredible. I felt no more arthritis and danced with my old buddy and I must say that I never felt so tipsy without one hard drink.

Pop and I are retired now. I always wondered what that would be like to suddenly not be involved in the costume business anymore. Our daughter Doris is now in charge and she is doing a good job. We are very proud of her.

Now we have time to take care of our little house and the garden and when we feel like it, we pack our RV and go see the rest of the United States. So I said, but Pop nixed that and replied that it would not be possible to see the entire United States, since it would take more than one life to do. Well, I said, "Okay then, at least as much as we can."

We have lived in this little house for over fifty years. I would not sell it now for a million dollars. It has too many memories. Mostly good.

Backyard

Chapter 28
A Note to the Family

There it is my whole life story. And to think that it all started after I found that empty ledger among my books while dusting.

I remember when I purchased the book. It was actually meant to be for all the different recipes for good bread I had collected over the years.

Every time I visited the old country, I admired the big variety of bread in bakery windows. Freshly baked in all forms and textures. Some were shaped into animals, like turtles, alligators, etc. Also gigantic pretzels for parties. I had seen some of those as large as a dining room table filled with cold meats, cucumbers, tomatoes, etc. cut into sandwiches for the guests to enjoy. Mostly on New Year's Eve.

On one of our last visits to Germany, my sister Charlott had quickly baked a bunch of long stemmed daisies and decided to arrange the pretty butter glazed "flowers" in a large white milk pitcher and then placed them right in the middle of the dining room table.

You could grab one of those beauties and spread each petal with butter or jelly. It was a nice conversation piece, pretty to look at and good to eat. I do not remember what we had for dinner that day, but I will always remember the bread daisies.

Maybe a bread book with illustrations would have been nice for Christmas or birthday presents or "just because" for somebody dear. (Maybe some other time).

Instead, I decided to write about my life and once I started, no one could stop me. Soon the ledger I had found was filled with stories. It was written in such a hurry since I was afraid this spell would not last. After all, it was such a long time ago but with a lot of determination, my German/English word processor and three years, "I did it!

The Family

It should have been that happy ending, but it was not to be. How could I exclude the hardest blow of my life? We'd counted our blessings and life was good for a long time. We lived in perfect harmony with our two children Mike and Doris. We also had six grandchildren; Benjie, David, Danny, Joline, Rob, and Mike; and three great grandchildren; Evan, Owen, and Hayden whom I proudly call, "The Future of America." Every one of them is a good-hearted character, bright and loving.

But, God gave us one more mountain to climb. We were informed that our son Mike had been diagnosed with cancer. After a nine-month battle, there was no more help for our boy and the terrible pain he endured, except morphine. It was sad to see him looking at his brand new boat knowing he didn't have many more chances to use it. When he did though, he and his new wife Milynn went fishing or crabbing. It was a pleasure to see them so happy. And, regardless of the pain, he continued to work. He was determined to finish what he had started and worked until the end. He died on March 25, 2001.

Four months later on July 27, 2001, my dear husband also left. He had a stroke while cutting the grass in the back yard while I was weeding in the front yard. I found him lying in a bed of flowers. Nothing could be done. He was gone. Both my son and husband are now together in Heaven. They are missed by many.

Rhine River castles, cathedrals and vineyards, near Bingen

164